Making
Gifts
for Men

Making Gifts for Men

BY SHIRLEY BOTSFORD

Photographs by Michael Weiss

Drawings by the author

DOUBLEDAY & COMPANY, INC., GARDEN CITY, NEW YORK

Library of Congress Cataloging in Publication Data

Botsford, Shirley J.
  Making gifts for men.

  1. Handicraft. 2. Gifts. I. Title. II. Title:
Gifts for men.
TT157.B696   1985   745.5   84-24660
ISBN 0-385-18543-X

Copyright © 1985 by Shirley Botsford
Printed in the United States of America
All Rights Reserved

Color insert designed by Joe Caroff.

Acknowledgment

I am dedicating *Making Gifts for Men* to all the men in my life who, over the years, have loved me despite the fact that they have not always loved the things that I have made for them. They have unknowingly provided me with the challenge and the motivation to write this book. To my father, James Botsford, who has generously filled my life with great ideas and unending inspiration; to my brother, Gary Botsford, because he always had an eye for quality and shared it with me; to Craig Merritt, who has constantly made me feel as if my talents are unlimited; and to Charles Walker, whose keen eye and precision work enabled him to find the only typographical mistake in the last book I wrote!

Notably, there are also a few great women who have contributed immensely to my success and provided the team needed to write *Making Gifts for Men*. To my mother, Ruth Jean Botsford, who has always insisted that it's better to do it yourself and then actually taught me all the skills I needed to know; to Pam Hoffman, who keeps me from making mistakes and whose steady hands and nimble fingers assisted me with every page; and to Marlene Connor, who turned the idea for this book into a reality.

As with all big projects, there are lots of people behind the scenes who have openly contributed their special talents to make it possible for me to write *Making Gifts for Men*. I would like to thank Marion Bartholomew, Helen Boyd, Tina Cantelmi, Nancy Cappuzzo, Mary DeVlieger, Vicki Entine, Casey Fuetsch, Elizabeth Ginsberg, Barbara Greenman, Scott Greenwald, Deborah Harding, Elfriede Hueber, Ann Karas, June King, Diana Klemin, Alexandra Kuman, Marie Lewis, Joy Margulis, Maureen McGee, Priscilla Miller, Suzanna Nickerson, Dawn Pinnock, Marion Patton, Mayme Sanders, Michael Vest, Diana Schlumpf, Michael Weiss, and Donna Wilder.

Contents

Introduction

There is at least one special man in almost everyone's life. Our healthy assortment of fathers, in-laws, brothers, friends, husbands, co-workers, uncles, sons, nephews, cousins, and grandfathers seems constantly to evoke our creative and nurturing instincts.

Everywhere I go I'm asked, "What can I make for a man? Why aren't there more projects for men in magazines and books?" We love to make things for our men. Some of us bake brownies and pies and cookies. As children we all proudly presented marvelous finger paintings and drawings as offerings of our great esteem.

Others write creatively scented letters, some take pictures of themselves to give and be cherished. A few even make taped cassettes of their feelings. As a last resort, a small minority might even send flowers or candy. This brings me to the reason for writing this book. We face a real challenge when selecting something to express our feelings to men. It becomes even more of a problem when you want to make something yourself.

In our enthusiasm we tend to overwork things, making them candidates for the back of the closet or the bottom of the *bottom* drawer or even a dark corner of the basement. How many of those items that we spent weeks (or months) making in secret have mysteriously gotten "lost" or "stolen" within days of their receipt? Have you heard this one—"Don't feel bad, it probably wouldn't have disappeared so fast if you hadn't done such a great job!"

It is safe to say that all of us instinctively know we must avoid the color hot pink when making something for a man. But we still try to put too much of ourselves into our gifts. The trick to making men's gifts that they will really want, like, use, enjoy, and possibly even wear out is to do lots of detective work.

The easy way out is to find out what he already has and really likes. Make it better in some way. If he loves plaid shirts, your best bet is to make a similar one in the best quality fabric you can find. Always use the best materials; your time is worth the investment. Make small samples of the technique and test materials so there will be no surprises after you've finished. Always preshrink fabrics.

Get to know his likes and dislikes well. Be sneaky, don't just machine-gun him with a bunch of questions. This will just make him suspicious, irritated, and *silent.* Besides, he probably doesn't even know what he likes, especially if you're planning something custom-made. He isn't aware of the great things that are possible by combining one's special skills and imagination, unless he is already making things for himself.

Observe him in action. What does he always do, wear, buy, use, show his friends, and, at the point of frustrating you beyond recovery, refuse to throw away? We are committed to what we like and what feels comfortable to us, not others, like the ragged blanket or teddy bear we had as kids. Be warned, these items can often be the most boring and least challenging things to make.

When he brings his favorite shirt to you for repairs as if it were a wounded puppy, take note. If you replace it with a new shirt that you think is cheery and different, your choice will probably never make it to the closet. If it doesn't disappear entirely, it may be found much later polishing the car or soaking up grease somewhere.

If you're making something for him to wear, recognize that you have accepted the supreme challenge. Do get the size right. Take into consideration how comfy and loose he likes his things. Measure something he has that is similar to what you're making and size it accordingly.

Lots safer than garments are things for him to use. Functional items are always the most appreciated. Useful things that save time, organize, solve a problem, or fill a need will be the most successful. I couldn't imagine anything to make that would be incredibly useful but never sees the light of day. Something utilitarian would thus be the safest idea for your first try. Remember, no matter what you select, consider it a challenge and be sure to do lots of research before beginning.

Hobbies are obvious hints. Try combining a technique that you enjoy with his favorite subject. "His and hers" stuff is usually a bad idea unless he suggests it. If he collects something, that's a good place to start. Just don't decoupage a rare stamp to a paperweight.

Show your idea to his friends. Get their reactions and suggestions. They will tend to be much more honest and straightforward than the recipient of the gift. This is also a good way to get some help and still keep things a surprise. Remember that the gift must look good to the man, and your feminine point of view is secondary.

Taking him with you to the fabric store to pick something out could mean a permanent change in the relationship. Usually this experience will drive you both crazy. If the smell of the freshly treated fabrics doesn't finish him, the overwhelming inventory will. Remember, stores are just not natural environments for men.

Select a few materials on your own. Ask for swatches or buy 1/8-yard pieces of some really good choices based on your previous "closet" research. Show him the swatches and get his opinion.

I've selected items for this book that would appeal to a wide variety of men. A lot of the items would be suitable for anyone, women included. If you know of an especially challenging type that hasn't been covered at all, I'd love to hear from you.

No matter what you decide to make, be sure you're willing to accept the challenge and possible failure and rejection. Men are the most discriminating consumers. Be willing to try again and again. Learn from your mistakes. You will know when you've succeeded because he will probably pay you the ultimate compliment in public by saying, "She made it for me."

Making
Gifts
for Men

1.

Getting Started

Gift Idea Questionnaire

At least once in his or her life almost everyone has found it impossible to figure out what gift to choose for someone special. It's apparently a common problem that becomes even more difficult when the gift needed is for a man. It seems to be really important to us to pick out the perfect present, but for lots of reasons we all too often run out of time and energy and ideas. We resort to the classic shirt or tie in desperation. I have put together this list of questions to help you think more creatively about gift-giving. I hope they will help you come up with a list of possibilities that will last a lifetime.

After you have asked yourself all the questions, look through the book and see if you can find a suitable project to make. Of course you will not be making every gift that you give, but the ones that you do make will be carefully thought out so that your time and efforts are well spent. The book is filled with a variety of projects, so all you have to do is find the right person to make them for.

Hobbies:

1. Does he have a hobby or has he expressed an interest in starting one?
2. Is there anything special that he always runs out of that you might get?

3. Has he ever mentioned something that he might like but is hesitant to splurge on himself?
4. Are there any items that he has been improvising without?
5. How is most of his free time spent?

Clothes:

1. Does he consider clothing to be a good gift?
2. Have you checked his closet to see what types of things he likes most?
3. What was the last thing that he bought for himself?
4. How loosely does he like his clothes to fit?
5. What are his favorite colors to *wear?*
6. Has he recently admired something that another man was wearing?
7. What kinds of fabrics does he prefer?
8. Has he recently lost or damaged anything that needs replacing?
9. Are practical things his favorite gifts?

Fun:

1. Would he really enjoy a joke gift?
2. Do you think he secretly might like you to throw a surprise party for him?
3. What is his most prized possession? Are there any accessories that could be added?

4. Does he appreciate your talents? Would he treasure something that you made simply for sentimental value?
5. What activities does he enjoy most?
6. Do you enjoy playing games like chess together?

Personal:

1. Does he like to receive photographs as gifts?
2. How does he feel about monograms or personalized items?
3. Could you help him break a bad habit by suggesting a new hobby, without offending him?
4. Has he mentioned having a pet and could you pick it out for him? Does his pet need something?
5. Are sports a main event in his life?
6. Is there something that would give his ego a boost?
7. Is he a happy homebody?

Services:

1. Would he appreciate it if you got someone to do one of his chores, such as mowing the lawn or shoveling snow?
2. Could you offer to help him with work or a big project and give him a ''coupon'' to redeem your services?
3. Does he have a favorite food that you could cook for him?

Business:

1. Does he need anything that just hasn't been in the budget?
2. Would organization be helpful?
3. Can you think of any timesavers?
4. What does a workaholic do to relax?
5. Does he travel?

Craft Supply Checklist

Assemble your tools and supplies in one place near your work area. Only a few basic supplies are needed for most craft projects. The right equipment, kept in a handy spot, will help you work quickly and efficiently. A large flat work area with good light is essential. Check the Project Directions for the specific supplies needed for each project.

Brown paper or shelf paper
Cardboard
Chalk pencils
Clear tape
Drafting compass
Hammer
Kneaded eraser
L-square or right triangle
Masking tape
Newspaper
Paper scissors
Pencil
Ruler
Sandpaper
Stick glue
Tracing paper
Utility knife
White glue

Sewing Supply Checklist

Choose your sewing supplies carefully so they do the job efficiently and wear well. A few well-chosen supplies will save time and steps, and you can do almost any sewing project with them. Organize the essentials near your sewing machine. Make sure you have a comfortable chair and good light. Refer to the Project Directions for the exact tools needed for each project.

Embroidery hoop
Fabric shears
Hand sewing needles
Pinking shears

Pointed embroidery scissors
Safety pins
Seam ripper
Steam iron
Straight pins
Tailor's chalk
Tape measure
Thimble
Thread
Zigzag sewing machine

General Notes

Instructions. Always read through all the instructions before you begin a project. This will give you a general understanding of the entire process and help you organize your work better. You will also find out what tools and materials to have ready so you won't need to interrupt progress to get things.

Supplies. A complete list of product sources and manufacturers is given at the back of the book. Use it to help locate materials and supplies that are unfamiliar to you. Definitions and descriptions of products used in this book are also given so that you can make substitutions where possible.

Terms. Often I find that the terms "lengthwise" and "crosswise" can cause confusion. For the instructions in this book, "lengthwise" always refers to the *longest* dimension. It also can indicate the fabric grain that runs parallel to the woven selvage edges. When "crosswise" is used, it always refers to the *shortest* dimension involved. The crosswise fabric grain runs across the fabric perpendicular to the selvage edges.

Sizing. Frequently it is necessary to custom-fit the projects that are to be worn. Schedule several fittings at important checkpoints as you need them. This can present a problem if you want the gift to be a surprise. As an alternative, simply take measurements from existing items that are similar to the project and estimate the dimensions. Always allow extra length or room to let something out. You can even baste seams where you anticipate adjustments will be needed, so that your alteration time is reduced later. Plan a fitting *after* you have given the gift to add any finishing touches.

▶ HINT. Take a full set of measurements at the fitting so you can use them for planning another surprise project.

Basic Sewing Techniques

Seam Allowance. A ½" seam allowance is used for all the sewing projects unless the directions indicate something different. Press all the seam allowances open except where directed otherwise.

Hand Sewing. Seams and all types of hand sewing should always be knotted in some way to prevent unraveling. For hand basting it is best to make a tiny back stitch rather than a knot. This permits the stitches to be removed quickly and easily.

Most hand sewing is started with a knot in the end of the thread. Snip the end of the thread that comes from the spool at an angle for easy threading. Don't ever break it or use your teeth to tear the thread. Thread the needle with this end, and pull about 12" to 18" of thread through the eye of the needle from the spool. Knot this same end of the thread as follows: Wrap the end of the thread around your index finger. Hold it in place and gently roll the thread between your forefinger and thumb. Slip this twisted loop off of your finger and pull it with your fingernail and thumbnail until a small knot is formed. Practice this a bit if you have never done it before. You will quickly be able to make tiny, tight, perfectly round little knots. Snip the thread coming from the spool about 6" from the needle. Thread inserted into a needle in this direction will knot and tangle less because the twist of the thread will be smoothed down as it is pulled through the fabric.

To finish off your hand sewing, first pull the needle to the wrong side of your work and take a tiny stitch (about 1/16" long) in the fabric. As your needle emerges from this stitch, wrap the thread that is closest to the needle tip around the point of the needle twice. Hold this wrapped thread with your thumb and pull the needle out of the fabric, through the loops of thread. Pull the knot slowly and snugly against the fabric. Submerge the end of the thread by taking a stitch between the layers of fabric that begins at the knot. Clip the thread off where it emerges from the fabric.

Machine Sewing. Be sure to always secure the thread ends whenever you stop stitching. This prevents the stitches from unraveling and adds to the overall stability of the project.

There are two ways to secure the thread end of machine-stitching. The first is to make 3 or 4 stitches in reverse at the beginning and end of seams or rows of stitching. This is called backtracking or security stitching. If your machine does not have a reverse stitch, you can make reverse stitches by beginning about 1/2" inside the raw edge. Sew toward the raw edge, stop at the edge, pivot your work around, and stitch back over the 1/2" of reverse stitching. Complete the seam. Pivot the work around and stitch back over the end of the seam for about 1/2".

The second method is used when stitching ends in the center of a piece of work, such as in machine quilting, where backtracking would be unattractive. It is important in this case to secure the ends of stitching invisibly. Stop stitching wherever you

like. Remove your work from the machine. Cut the threads about 6" or 8" from the stitching. Turn your piece over and pull the bobbin thread gently. A loop will appear. Insert a pin into this loop and pull the upper thread through to the back of the work. Tie the bobbin thread and the upper thread together with a square knot. Insert both ends into a needle. Hide the thread ends by inserting the needle back into the fabric. Emerge about 1" away. Remove the needle and snip the thread ends close to the fabric. The knot and thread ends will be almost undetectable.

Bias Strips. True bias strips are cut from fabric yardage for use as binding or piping. You can buy bias tape and piping in a limited number of solid colors and a few prints. If you want to use a special fabric or need to match an unusual color, you will want to cut your own bias strips.

Make sure you have at least 1 yard of the fabric that you want to use. Straighten the cut edge of the fabric. Illustration A on page opposite.

Fold the yardage diagonally, bringing the raw straightened edge of the fabric to meet the selvage of the fabric. A perfect 45-degree angle is formed by the fold that results. Pin the straightened edge of the fabric to the selvage. Crease the fabric at the fold. Cut along the crease.

Draw lines 2" away from and parallel to the fold line that you have cut. Pin the 2 layers of fabric together to prevent slipping when you cut out the 2" strips. Measure the length of the bias strips and cut out as many as you will need to complete your project. Illustration B on page opposite.

Sew these bias strips together by making a diagonal seam as follows: Place the right sides of the fabric together and match the short edges. The strips should form a right angle as they are put together because of the 45-degree angled edge at the short end of each strip. Pin and stitch a seam

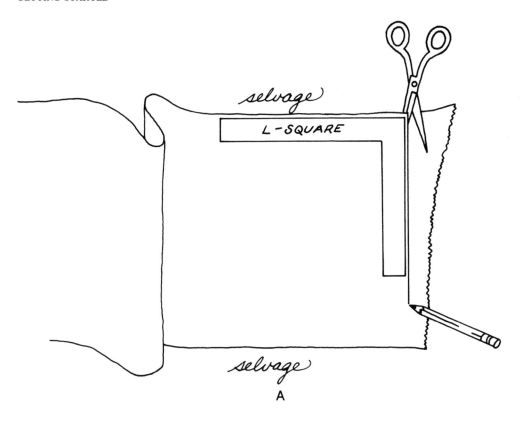

selvage

L-SQUARE

selvage

A

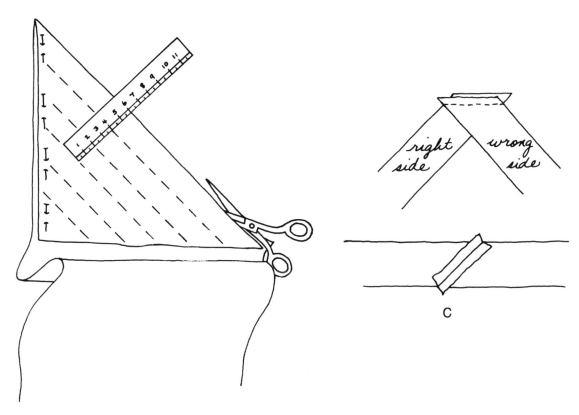

right
side

wrong
side

B

C

½" away from the short edges. The seam should follow the grain of the fabric. Press the seam open. Illustration C on page 5.

Overcasting. Any stitch that wraps or covers a raw edge with thread can be considered overcasting. The purpose of this stitching is to finish the raw seam edges and prevent them from unraveling when the items are used and washed. Overcasting seams lengthens the life of an item and makes it neatly finished inside. It doesn't take much additional time at all, so it is well worth the effort.

The zigzag stitch is the most commonly used for overcasting. The newer home sewing machines have lots of fancy stitches. Some of them make overlock and merrow stitches similar to the ones you find in manufactured clothing. Any of these could be used for overcasting. Some are only suitable for particular kinds of fabrics. Check your owner's manual for suggestions.

Trimming Seam Allowances. Seams often overlap when pieces of fabric are joined together, especially in patchwork. This overlapping of layers can cause bumps and ridges on the right side of your work. Often these bumps and ridges don't show up until it is pressed, worn, or laundered. To eliminate this problem, remember to trim the corners of the seam allowances diagonally. This minimizes the bump at the intersection of the seam.

Drawing Circles. Many of the craft projects in this book use circles as patterns. Use a compass to draw small circles. Large circles can be drawn in two ways. The first method uses a common round object such as a plate, skillet lid, or pizza pan. Place the object flat on the pattern paper. Hold it down with one hand and draw around it with the other. Remove the object and cut the circle out. Fold it in half, mark the fold line, and measure the diameter of the

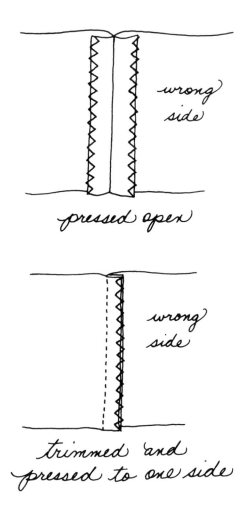

wrong side

pressed open

wrong side

trimmed and pressed to one side

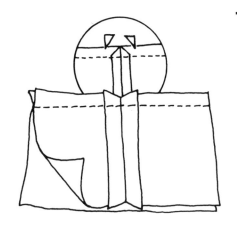

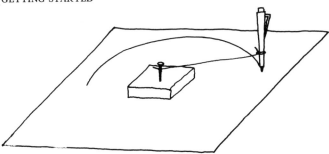

circle. The size of the circle can be decreased or increased as needed by adding or subtracting an even amount around the entire circumference of the circle.

The second method (above) uses a felt tip pen, string, and a nail. Tape newspaper sections together to make one piece large enough for the circle you need to draw. Drive the nail into a small scrap piece of wood and center it on the newspaper. Tie the end of the string to the pen. Divide the circle diameter in half. Cut the string to this measurement plus about 3″ for tying. Tie the cut end to the nail and adjust it so that the distance between the pen and the nail is equal to the radius of the circle. Weight the scrap wood down so that it doesn't move. Extend the pen out to the full length of the string. Adjust the string so it is held parallel to the ground. Draw the entire circle around the nail, keeping the string taut and pen absolutely vertical.

Flat-fell Seam. This is a strong, durable type of seam that is easy to do. It has the advantage of being self-finished so that no raw edges or seam allowances are visible on either side. This is probably the flattest and most rugged seam, making it especially suitable for men's projects. The seam is made on the right side of the fabric and also provides an extra decorative, professional touch. Practice this seam on scrap fabric before using it on your project.

Match the wrong sides of the fabric along the edges to be seamed together. This finish is not suitable for extremely curved seams.

Stitch the seam ½″ from the raw edges. Press the seam open. Trim one of the seam allowances down to ⅛″. Press ⅛″ over along the edge of the larger seam allowance toward the side facing you. Fold the larger seam allowance over the trimmed seam allowance, encasing all the raw edges. Pin and then topstitch the folded edge flat in place. Two rows of stitching, spaced ¼″ apart, are visible on the right side. Keep your stitching as straight as possible. All the seams in a project should be of uniform width.

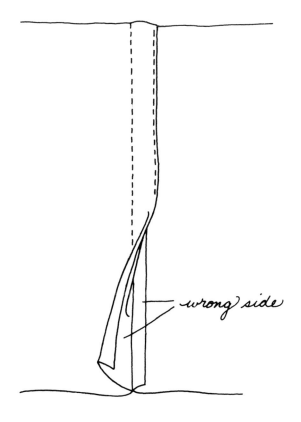

wrong side

Topstitching. Large, straight machine-stitching is made from the right side of the fabric for both decorative and functional purposes. Set your machine to make 6 to 10 stitches per inch. Special thread is available for decorative topstitching that is heavier than normal sewing thread. If this is not available, you can use 2 spools of regular thread in the same color. Refer to the sewing machine manual and set your machine up to accommodate 2 spools of thread. Use the 2 strands of thread as 1. A slightly larger machine needle may be necessary. Test the topstitching on scrap fabric and make tension adjustments if necessary.

Vinyl Sewing. Clear plastic and vinyl require special handling to ensure good results. The slick surface of the material may stick to the flatbed and presser foot of the machine. To eliminate this problem, cut strips of tissue paper and place them over the area that's creating a problem as you stitch. You can see through the paper and it is easily torn away without a trace after the stitching is finished. Wax paper can also be used if the tissue paper tears too easily. Use inexpensive white, translucent tissue that comes folded in packages. To easily cut many strips at once, draw lines spaced 1″ apart across the folded end. Cut on the lines through all the layers at one time.

Straight pins leave holes in the vinyl and are often difficult to insert. Use paper clips or masking tape to hold the layers together for stitching. A special wedge-shaped machine needle can help make stitching easier. Use 8 to 10 stitches per inch. Tie off the thread ends rather than backtracking. Trim all seam allowances to ¼″ and use your fingers to crease the seam allowances in one direction. Do not iron plastic or vinyl.

Monograms

Add a Personal Accent to Almost Any Gift

Personalized gifts are often the most popular items for the giver as well as the receiver, and they are fun to do. With the simple addition of a name or initials you can turn an ordinary gift into something really special. If you have never made anything before, this is a great way to get started. There are lots of quick and easy techniques for adding letters to an item that you have made or purchased.

Ideas for customizing your gifts can be found everywhere. Almost any store or shop that you visit will carry at least one personalized item. Magazines and mail order catalogues frequently feature merchandise that you can special order. There are also lots of businesses that offer monogramming, engraving, or printing services when you buy their products. These are all great sources for ideas and, possibly, some terrific gifts. Simply by being observant you will find yourself coming up with ideas for personalized projects to make yourself.

This chapter includes all the basic information for monogramming and lots of exciting ideas. These techniques can also be used to add initials to almost every project in the book. Handmade gifts become a real keepsake when you embellish them with a personalized accent. Check the color pages for some examples of personalized projects that I'm sure you'll want to make. I liked a few so much that I couldn't resist putting my *own* initials on some of my favorites.

Supplies and Sources for Letters

Alphabets. When you plan to create a monogram with paint, embroidery, or some other craft technique, you will need an alphabet in the right size. If you're lucky, sometimes you can trace letters that are just right for your project out of a newspaper or magazine. Unfortunately, space limitations keep me from including alphabets in this book, so I have suggested lots of good sources.

Try to find lettering in the same size that is needed. Sometimes it is hard to locate the letters you want in the right size. Simple letters are easy to enlarge slightly. Merely extend the straight ends of each letter evenly, using a ruler and pencil. Avoid changing the letter size drastically yourself. It is necessary to size them proportionally. A photostat shop can enlarge or reduce it to your specifications. They can easily make several sizes so you can choose what looks best.

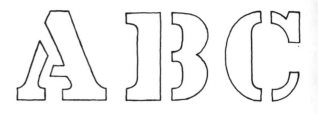

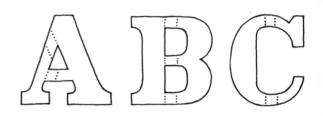

1. **Books and Booklets.** Many needlework books contain alphabets that can be used for a variety of embroidery techniques, including cross-stitch and needlepoint. Check your library for these as well as books on lettering, typography, and advertising production techniques.

▶ HINT. An alphabet I use frequently came from the ABC book I had as a child.

2. **Stencils.** Inexpensive paper and plastic stencils are widely available in stationery, hardware, variety, and art material stores. They come in a big selection of sizes and styles. The Roman and Gothic styles are the easiest to work with.

▶ HINT. Stencil letters contain tiny paper bridges that hold the parts of the letter in place. They have a stenciled look and are not usually included in a monogram. To remove them, draw the letter on a plain piece of paper. Erase the stencil bridges and reconnect the outlines of the letter to form a solid shape.

3. **Stick-on Letters.** These are available in a variety of plastics, papers, and metals. They are suitable only for hard, nonwashable items. They have a sticky back that adheres to a clean surface when pressed in place. It is a good idea to use glue to apply this type of letter if durability is expected.

▶ HINT. Carefully apply a coat of clear nail polish over each letter for an extra long-wearing finish.

4. **Iron-on Fabric Letters.** These are cut-out fabric letters that have a fusible material on the back. A good assortment of sizes, colors, and textures can be found in fabric or hobby stores. Machine-embroidered monograms are also available with a fusible backing to iron on for a simulated hand-embroidered look. Follow the manufacturer's directions carefully. Always use a press cloth to protect your iron from the fusing materials. Check the care instructions before laundering.

▶ HINT. Stitching by hand or machine around the outer edges of an iron-on let-

ter will prevent it from peeling off due to
wear. Use a contrasting thread color and
a fancy stitch for an added decorative
outline effect.

5. *Heat Transfer Letters.* These alphabets are made of a synthetic bonding
   material applied to a paper backing.
   The letters are backward. They are
   usually available in assorted sizes of
   black, white, and red. Follow the manufacturer's directions carefully. Before
   beginning, always test one letter on
   scrap fabric or in a spot where it won't
   show. Work carefully because these letters cannot be removed after they are
   transferred.

► HINT.   Use fabric pens or permanent
felt tip markers to add colorful decorative
outlines or drawings around the transferred
letters.

Basic Techniques for Using Letters

1. *Positioning Letters.* Monograms become an attractive accent when you
   follow a few simple guidelines for proper
   placement. Make sure that the letters
   are centered and in a straight line. Mark
   a baseline and a center point on your
   project with chalk or tape that can be
   easily removed later. Align the baseline
   of the letters to the baseline on the project. Position the letters evenly on each
   side of the center point. Keep them well
   spaced. Generally about one quarter of
   the letter width is good.

With the exception of the iron-on or
stick-on letters, it is necessary to make a
working pattern. This is the layout of the letters as you want them to appear on the
finished project. Draw a baseline on a
separate piece of plain paper. Trace each
letter onto this line, placing the bottom
edges directly on the line. Use the traced

layout as your working pattern for transferring to the project.

► HINT.   Sometimes it is difficult to
decide where you would like to place your
monogram. To test placement, draw the
letters on paper and cut them out. Place
them in all the possible positions and select
the spot you like best. If the project is a garment, be sure to try it on for the placement
test.

2. *Transferring Designs.* Select a piece of
   dressmaker's carbon paper in a color
   that will show up well on the project.
   Cut a piece slightly larger than the
   monogram. Slip it under the preposi-
   tioned monogram working pattern with
   the carbon side against the project.
   Work on a hard, flat surface. Hold all
   the layers in place securely as you draw
   over the letter outlines. The drawn lines
   will be transferred to the project. Check
   to see if it transferred well before removing the working pattern.

If you are working on a light-colored
material, such as a white shirt or handkerchief, the monogram can be traced directly
onto the project. Find a bright window that
is at a convenient working height. If necessary, go over the outlines of the letters to
make them as dark as possible.

Tape the working pattern to the window.
With the right side toward you, place the
material over the design so that the placement is correct. Tape the material to the
window. Using a sharp, soft pencil, trace
the letters onto the right side of the fabric.
If you have a table with a glass or plexiglass
top, you will find it easier to work on. Place
a light on the floor beneath the table and
proceed as just described.

New design-transferring products are ap-
pearing on the market constantly. Check
your local sewing and art supply shops.
One good product is a design transfer pencil. With it, you trace the letters onto the

back of the working pattern so they appear backward. This side is positioned and then ironed onto the material. Test these products before using them on your project and be sure to follow the instructions carefully.

► **HINT.** Craft and pattern companies carry iron-on transfer patterns for letters and designs. You simply cut them out, position them, and iron them onto the material. Definitely worth a try!

Hand-Embroidered Monograms

Almost any garment will acquire a bit of prestige by the addition of a beautiful hand-embroidered monogram. It is a really relaxing hobby that requires only a few simple supplies: scissors, embroidery needles, a small embroidery hoop, a thimble, and 6-strand embroidery floss in a color that goes well with the fabric.

► **HINT.** Basting a small piece of fabric, such as organdy, to the wrong side of the work will stabilize it. This makes the stitching go a lot easier and the finished monogram will look neater. Special fabrics are made specifically for this purpose, but any lightweight interfacing or crisp, tightly woven fabric will do. A ¼-yard piece will be enough for about 4 to 6 monograms.

Transfer the monogram to the right side of the fabric. Clear an area on the garment about 2″ larger than your embroidery hoop so it is easy to insert. This may involve opening a seam partially.

Cut a piece of stabilizer fabric that is about 2″ larger than your hoop. Center this under the spot where the monogram will be placed and baste it in place. Working from the right side, place basting stitches around each letter, securing the fabric to the stabilizer. Insert the 2 layers into the hoop together.

For embroidering a pocket, completely remove the pocket from the garment. Baste it to your stabilizer fabric and then insert it into the hoop. Remember to note how the pocket was attached so you can replace it in the same manner.

Cut a 12″ to 18″ length of 6-strand floss. Separate this into 2 lengths that have 3 strands each. Insert one length into your needle. Rather than knotting one end, take several tiny stitches on the wrong side of your work. Hold a 2″-end of thread on the back until your first few embroidery stitches have held it in place.

A satin stitch is worked from one edge of the letter to the other. Decide in which direction you would like to place the stitches. Generally it looks best if all the stitches go in one direction. Fill in the entire letter with stitching. To end, take several tiny back stitches on the wrong side and sink the thread end into the work.

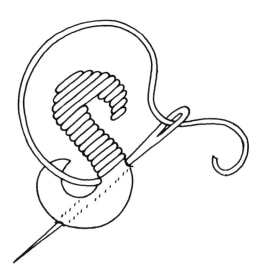

A tiny outline stitch can be worked around the entire letter. This adds a decorative edge and also helps to visually straighten any unevenness in the satin stitches. Simple outlined letters are extra

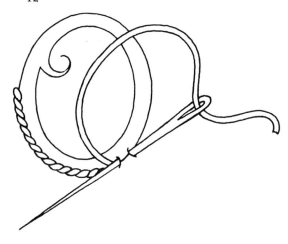

fast if you want to omit the satin stitching altogether. Work outline stitching over the letter outline and leave the fabric showing in between.

► **HINT.** If this is your first try at hand embroidery, work up some confidence by polishing your technique. Put this practice to good use by working your samples on a set of pillow cases for yourself.

Remove all the basting. Carefully trim the stabilizer fabric away ¼" around the wrong side of the monogram. Put a folded terry cloth towel on your ironing board. Place the right side of the monogram face down on the towel. Steam press on a setting that is appropriate for the fabric. Restitch the garment seams if necessary.

Machine-Appliquéd Letters

With a bit of practice you can turn your zigzag sewing machine into a monogrammer. It is a skill well worth learning because it takes only minutes to do each letter. You will need basic sewing supplies, a firmly woven fabric for the letters, and a small piece of fusible web material.

► **HINT.** Try using a striped or checked fabric for the letters. Experiment with different fabric colors and textures. For example, cut out a corduroy letter held

diagonally on the ribs of the fabric. Then stitch it down on the same fabric with the ribs going in a different direction.

First, transfer the letters to the right side of the fabric. Because you will be working with such small cutout letters, it is essential to use a fusible material to secure them in place before stitching. Place the fusing material against the wrong side of the fabric directly behind the letters. Baste the two layers together inside the outline of the letter and use them as one piece.

Cut the letters out ⅛" outside their outlines. You will be cutting the fuser and the fabric at the same time. The ⅛" border allows room for the machine satin stitching. Position the letters and pin them in place. Working on your ironing board, cover the letters with a press cloth. *Lightly* steam them in place. Lift the press cloth and carefully remove all pins and basting. Cover again and press well, following the manufacturer's instructions. Allow the letters to cool before moving them.

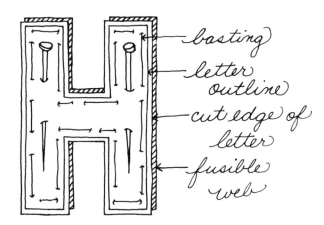

Consult your sewing machine manual and set your machine to closely spaced zigzag stitches that are about ⅛" wide. Adjust the thread tension so it is looser than normal. Make a test on scrap fabric.

Center the machine zigzag satin stitching

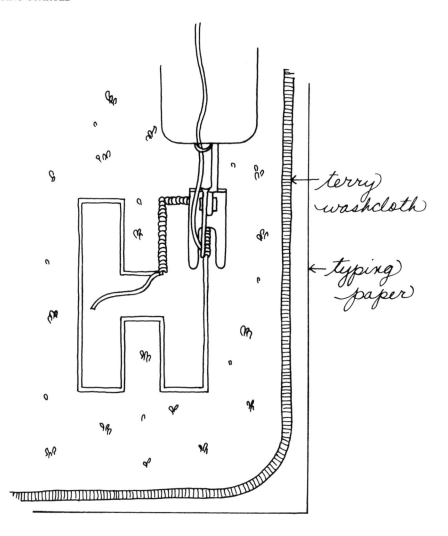

terry washcloth

typing paper

over the fabric raw edges. If your fabrics are lightweight, you may notice some puckering. To prevent this and allow for easy turning around curves, place one or two sheets of typing paper under your work, next to the machine. Satin stitch through the fabric and paper (above). Tie all thread ends securely. Tear the paper away when all the stitching is completed.

To ensure even, neat corners, turn the appliqué letter by removing the machine needle and then recentering the satin stitches over the raw edges.

► Hint. Do a bit of practicing on a set of towels and washcloths appliquéd for yourself. The terry cloth provides an excellent surface that doesn't reveal the tiny technical imperfections that naturally occur when you're learning. Even a crooked line will not show on terrycloth.

Look through your sewing machine manual carefully. The capabilities of sewing machines vary quite a bit. The manual will contain additional information on any special embroidery techniques that your machine can do.

2.

Make It to Get Personal

PROJECT

Personalize Accessories Instantly—Use Stick-on Letters

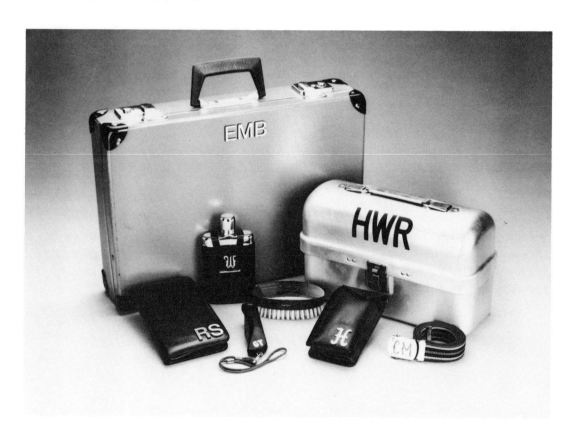

MATERIALS:

1 gift item, such as a manicure set, hair brush, flask, metal lunch box, pocket knife, or briefcase.

Stick-on initials in metal or plastic or paper

DIRECTIONS:

Placement. Generally, letters look best centered on an object. Place the letters in different spots to decide what you like best. No matter where they are placed, make sure the initials are straight. Use a ruler to mark a baseline, if necessary, with chalk or masking tape that can be removed later. Also indicate the center point of the object. Refer to Chapter 1 for specific information on using letters.

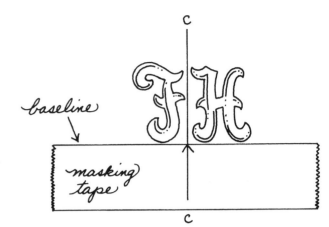

Letters. Follow the manufacturer's instructions carefully for applying the letters. Put the middle letter down first at the center point. Space the other 2 letters evenly to the left and right of the center letter. If you are using only 2 letters, space them equally on each side of the center point.

▶ **HINT.** Select letters that go well with the object on which you are placing them. A good general rule is to put paper on paper items, plastic on inexpensive or functional items, and metal (or metallic-looking plastic) on leather or more expensive things.

Beach Towel with a Quick Iron-on Message

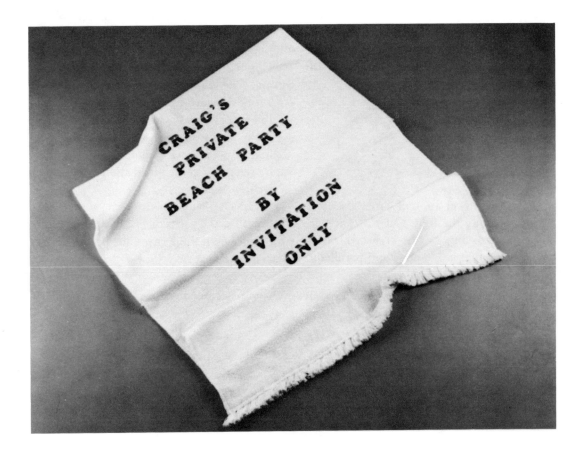

MATERIALS:

1 plain beach towel
1½" precut iron-on fabric letters in a contrasting color (get enough to spell out
   your message)

DIRECTIONS:

Placement. Write your own message out on a piece of paper, placing it in lines as you would like it to appear on the towel. Count the number of lines needed. Count how many of each letter you will need. Often one package of letters contains only one alphabet. You will probably need extra vowels. The number of letters needed to spell out "Private Beach Party—By Invitation Only" is given below. Don't forget to also add the letters for the name you are using.

A — 4	I — 4	P — 2
B — 2	L — 1	R — 2
C — 1	N — 3	T — 4
E — 2	O — 2	V — 2
H — 1		Y — 3

Fold the towel in half crosswise and crease it along the fold. Open it out flat. Draw a chalk line on the crease. Draw a second line that is 3″ above and parallel to the first line. Draw as many lines as are needed for your message. If you are using a lot of words, you will need to draw lines above and below the center line. Draw 7 lines to do the beach towel as shown. Leave one line blank between the words "Party" and "By".

Lettering. Follow the manufacturer's instructions for using the letters. Test one letter on a scrap before beginning. Fold the towel in half lengthwise and draw a chalk line marking the center as you did before. Count the letters and spaces in each row and start with the center letter of each line. Work outward to the left and right. Space the letters evenly, about ¼″ apart. Leave a 1½″ space between words. Before pressing, double-check each letter for accuracy by referring to the illustration or your own written message.

► HINT. Make your own giant beach towel from 2 yards of 44″-wide terry cloth. Simply hem the 2 raw ends before adding your message.

Hand-Embroidered Monogramming for Purchased Ties

MATERIALS:

1 plain or subtly patterned tie made from a smooth, tightly woven fabric.
6-strand embroidery floss in a coordinating color
¼ yard interfacing to use as a stabilizer
Alphabet to transfer

DIRECTIONS:

Placement. Use removable chalk to mark a baseline for the letters 1½″ to 2″ above the larger, pointed end of the tie. Also mark the center of the tie on the baseline. Make a working pattern for the letters. Center and transfer it to the baseline, following instructions.

Embroidery. Carefully open the seam of the tie far enough so that the area to be embroidered can be opened out flat. Baste the fabric stabilizer to the wrong side of the tie and continue as described under Hand Embroidered Monograms in Chapter 1. After you complete the embroidery, restitch the seam.

► **HINT.** Hand-embroidered monograms will elegantly enhance simple items like shirts, pajamas, bathrobes, scarves, and handkerchieves. Try your hand at adding initials to a purchased tie for a very special custom-made look. Use a counted cross-stitch alphabet to embroider initials on a linen tie. The tie is cut on the bias so the letters will be worked diagonally. Prepare the tie for embroidery as just described. Work the middle letter first, centering it diagonally on the grain line of the tie.

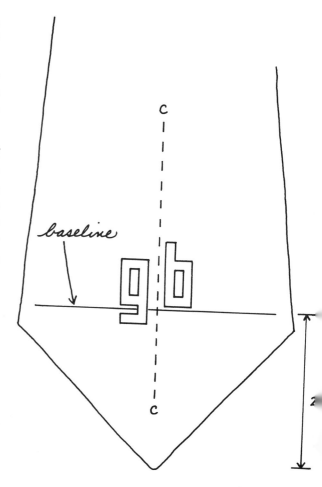

Gift Wrap and Ribbon to Make with Rubber Stamps

MATERIALS:

Plain brown kraft paper, white shelf paper, or decorative paper—1 roll or sheets
  large enough to wrap the gift planned
Fabric or craft ribbon in a plain color wide enough to accommodate the stamp
Letter and/or design rubber stamps
Stamp pad and brown stamp pad ink (refiller)

DIRECTIONS:

Rubber Stamp. A variety of decorative rubber stamps is readily available in novelty, stationery, and toy stores. Pick out a boat, train, plane, or similar subject that might appeal to a man. Personalize it even further by selecting something that relates to his job or hobby. Letters are also available in printing sets made for children. Your local rubber stamp company can even custom-make a special design for you. Stamps are fun to use on any paper item. Try your hand at transforming an ordinary object into a treasured gift for someone really special.

Placement. Test wrap your gift as you normally would, using a piece of newspaper. Carefully unwrap the gift without tearing the paper. Flatten it out and use this as a pattern to cut out a piece of paper for stamping.

Repeat the rubber stamp in rows to make an allover design. Draw guidelines very lightly on the paper so they can be erased later. The rows can be horizontal, vertical, or diagonal. Measure the width of the stamp (or combined letter stamps) and add 1". This is the *stamp width* needed between each guideline. Measure the height of the stamp and add 1" to find the *stamp height*.

Locate the center of the paper. Use a yardstick to draw one vertical and one horizontal line that intersect perpendicularly at the center point. Draw a line parallel to the vertical line that is placed the *stamp width* distance away. Continue drawing parallel lines in this way until the paper is completely covered. Repeat this with the horizontal lines, using the *stamp height* for spacing. The entire piece of paper will be covered with a lightly drawn grid.

For a diagonal design, turn the paper so it is placed at an angle facing you. Draw a vertical line that connects 2 opposite corners. Draw a horizontal line that is perpendicular to the vertical line. The horizontal line will not necessarily connect the 2 remaining corners. Cover the paper with a grid as just described.

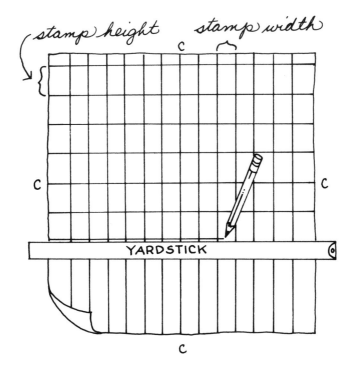

Stamping. Work on a hard, flat surface covered with newspaper. Hold the paper and the stamp in an upright position while working. Press the rubber stamp on the stamp pad, moistening the design surface with ink. Lift and immediately center the stamp inside one of the grid boxes near the edge of the paper. Press it down firmly without moving in any other direction. Any sideways movement can cause you to print a double image or blurred design. Hold for a second and lift the stamp directly off the paper vertically. Keep your fingers clear of the paper to prevent smearing.

Repeat this, working around the edge of the paper and then moving to the center. This will give you some practice before continuing into the center area, which will show the most when the package is wrapped. Use a kneaded eraser to remove the lines without leaving a trace.

More than one letter can be stamped at the same time. Arrange the letter stamps in the proper order. Lay them down next to each other on the table. Use masking tape to secure them together. Make sure that the stamping surface of each letter is even with the next. Use a rubber band over the tape to hold them tightly in position. Use the combined letters as one stamp.

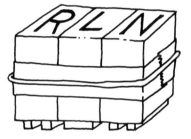

► **HINT.** My friends always make fun of me because I carefully unwrap my presents and save the paper. It's very likely that your hand-stamped paper will be cherished. Put it to good use later by covering a small juice can to use as a pencil holder.

Ribbon. Test wrap the gift with string to determine how much ribbon must be stamped. Measure the string and add a length of at least 24 " to make a nice bow. Cut a piece of ribbon to this measurement. Begin at one end of the ribbon and stamp the design in a continuous pattern. Leave about 1 " of space between stampings.

Stationery with Simple Stamped Designs

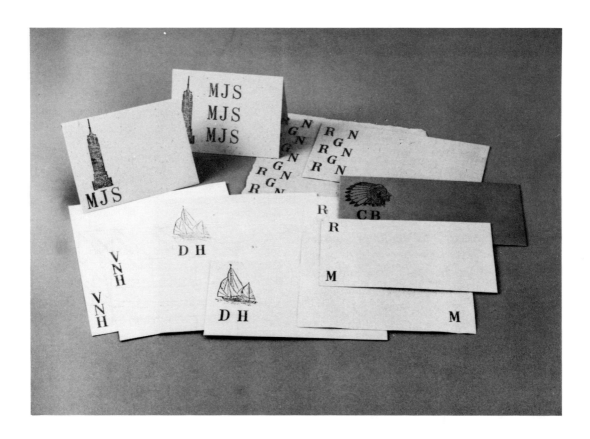

MATERIALS:

1 box plain paper and envelopes in a subtle color or texture
Letter and/or design rubber stamps
Stamp pad and brown stamp pad ink (refiller)

DIRECTIONS:

Placement. Generally, designs look best when positioned at the top edge of the stationery and envelopes. One stamp is enough when placed in the upper left-hand corner. Rows of stamps also look great across the top or along the side edge. If you are stamping repeatedly on the same sheet, refer to the placement directions under Gift Wrap and Ribbon.

Test your ideas before stamping the stationery. Cut a few bond paper shapes to match the stationery and envelope sizes. Use these to experiment with the placement of the stamps. After selecting the one you like best, lightly draw a baseline in the same location on each piece.

Stamping. Stamp each piece, referring to the stamping directions under Gift Wrap and Ribbon. Allow them to dry thoroughly before stacking them.

► **HINT.** If the recipient of this gift likes to do things himself, give it to him wrapped as a kit. It's a simple project that would make a great vacation or get-well project. Just include stationery, practice paper, and a personalized rubber stamp and pad. Adding a pen and a few postage stamps might improve your chances of getting a nice note!

Paper Portfolio for Filing Important Papers

MATERIALS:

Heavy cardboard—2 pieces 12" × 16"
Decorative paper—2 sheets 16" × 20"
2"-wide brown cloth tape—1 roll or 4 yards
2 yards 1"-wide brown grosgrain ribbon
Heavy paper for lining to coordinate with the decorative paper and tape—2 sheets
    11" × 15"
White glue
Rubber stamp and stamp pad (optional)

DIRECTIONS:

Cardboard Covers. Cut the cardboard and papers to the dimensions given in the materials list. Working flat, place one piece of decorative paper right side down. Thin a small amount of glue with an equal amount of water. Stir well and use a brush to evenly coat one side of the cardboard. Center the glued side of the cardboard on the wrong side of the paper. Press it flat, cover with a piece of wax paper, and weight it down evenly with books. Repeat this to make the other side of the portfolio. Allow them to dry overnight.

Fold each corner of the paper to the un-covered side of the cardboard. Glue them in place. Fold the side edges of the paper over and glue them in place. You will have formed a miter at each corner. Weight the pieces down as before and allow to dry.

► HINT.   If you haven't got time to wait for the glue to dry, make a portfolio in no time by using adhesive paper. Cut the pieces for the cover and the lining as given. Assemble the portfolio in the same way, omitting the gluing steps.

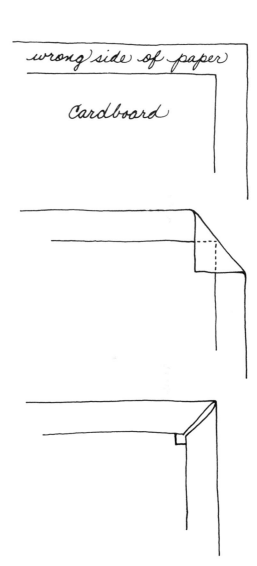

Taped corners. Cut a 6" length of tape. On the right side, center it over one corner so the edge of the tape extends ½" beyond the point. Press the ½" extension to the wrong side. Wrap the ends of the tape around the cardboard corner, forming a miter on the wrong side. Repeat this on the corner adjacent to the first on one *long* side of the cover. Make a second cover in the same manner.

Taped Spine. Cut a 20" length of tape. Lay it down on a flat surface with the sticky side up. With the *wrong* side up, position the plain long edge of one cover on the tape. Place it so it overlaps ½" onto the tape. The tape will extend about 2" on each end. Position the second cover in the same manner so about ½" of tape remains exposed between the covers. Fold the ends of the tape to the inside. Cut a 16" length of tape and center it over the covers and taped spine. Press it in place.

Turn the portfolio over. Cut a 20" length of tape. Center this on one cardboard side of the portfolio so the edge is even with the edge of the cardboard. Repeat on the opposite side. Turn the portfolio so the wrong side is up. Fold the ends of the tape to the inside.

Ribbon. Cut six 12" lengths of ribbon. Mark the center point on each long and short edge of the portfolio. Using the glue full strength, attach one piece of ribbon to each mark so 1" extends onto the wrong side of the cardboard. Allow to dry well.

Lining. Brush diluted glue onto the wrong side of one cover. Center the heavy paper on top, concealing all the paper, ribbon, and tape edges. Repeat this on the other side, weight it down, and allow to dry as before.

Stamping. Center one stamp on the right side of the portfolio, placing it 1" below the ribbon on the long edge.

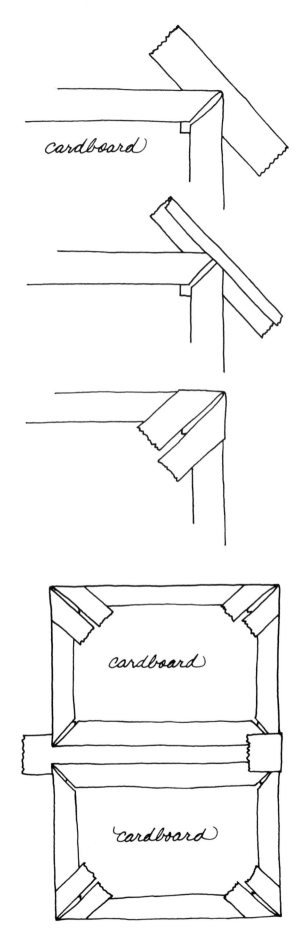

cardboard

cardboard

cardboard

Journals to Cover and Personalize

MATERIALS:

1 small blank paper notebook
Decorative paper
¼ yard adhesive paper in a pattern or texture
White glue
Rubber stamp and pad (optional)

DIRECTIONS:

Covering. Measure the front and back cover of the book. Add 2 " to the length and width measurements. Cut 2 pieces of decorative paper to these dimensions. Follow the gluing instructions under the previous project—Paper Portfolio. Apply glue to the front cover. Position the paper so it is centered with one long edge even with the edge of the spine. Fold the corners to the inside of the cover and glue as explained under the Paper Portfolio. Repeat this on the back cover.

Corners. Cut four 1½" × 3" strips from the adhesive paper. Peel off the paper backing and apply one to each outer corner of the front and back covers as described under the Paper Portfolio.

Spine. Cut a 3"-wide strip of adhesive paper that is the same length as the front cover length. Peel off the backing. Center this on the spine, matching the top and bottom edges. With the book closed, fold the edges to the front and back covers. "Burnish" the adhesive paper with a soft cloth so it will stick very well.

Inside cover. Subtract ¼" from the length and width of the cover dimensions. Cut 2 pieces of adhesive paper to this size. Apply them to the front and back inside covers, concealing all the paper edges.

Stamping. Follow the stamping instructions under Gift Wrap to decorate the paper covers as desired.

► Hɪɴᴛ. Make a matched set of these volumes in different sizes for an impressive gift. They're perfect for artists, authors, students, and any serious note-takers.

Terry Bathwrap with Appliquéd Initials

MATERIALS:

44"-wide red terry cloth (enough for 2 bathwraps) small—½ yards, medium—1¾ yards, large—1⅞ yards
1 yard 1"-wide elastic
¼ yard black 1"-wide Velcro
1½ yards ½"-wide black bias tape
Black broadcloth—approximately 4" × 6" for letters
3" Gothic letter stencils
Fabric fuser—4" × 6"
Black and red thread

DIRECTIONS:

Cutting. The bathwrap instructions are given in 3 waist sizes: small (28"–32"), medium (34"–38"), and large (40"–44"). Spread the fabric out flat. Straighten the ends of the fabric if necessary. Along one selvage edge, cut a rectangle that measures 22" × 52" (small), 22" × 58" (medium), or 22" × 64" (large). Do not trim off the selvage.

Stripes and Letters. The bathwrap closes left over right. With the selvage at the top, draw 2 vertical chalk lines 1½" from the left edge, spaced 1" apart. They will be parallel to the left edge. Cut two 22" pieces of bias tape. Baste one piece next to each chalk line. Using black thread, center a ⅛"-wide, closely spaced zigzag stitch over each bias tape edge.

Apply 2 black broadcloth letters to the bathwrap, referring to Machine-Appliquéd Letters in Chapter 1.

The letters are placed 2" up from the hem edge and ½" to the right of the stripes.

Assembly. Separate the 2 sides of the Velcro. Both pieces are applied to the right side of the fabric. Machine stitch one piece on the left side of the wrap ¾" away from and parallel to the selvage edge. On the right-hand side stitch the other Velcro piece 2½" away from and parallel to the selvage.

Overcast the two 22" ends of the wrap. Press ½" to the wrong side. Straight stitch the narrow hem in place ¼" from the fold. Hem the bottom raw edge of the wrap in the same manner.

Make a 2¼"-wide casing at the top edge by pressing the selvage edge to the wrong side of the fabric. Pin the casing along the fabric selvage. Mark points 12" from each end of the wrap. Leave openings at these spots to allow for elastic insertion. Machine straight stitch the casing in place.

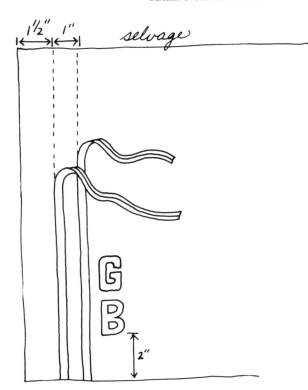

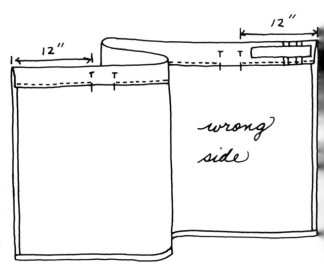

Draw a chalk line that divides the casing in half lengthwise. Pin and stitch along
this line, beginning and ending at the elastic
openings. Cut the elastic in half. Use a
large safety pin to insert one piece into each
channel of the casing. Securely machine
stitch across the elastic ends through all
thicknesses on one side of the wrap. Pull
the elastic up until the total waist casing
measurement is 44″ (small), 50″ (medium),
or 56″ (large). Trim off any excess elastic
and machine-stitch the ends as before.

Optional Pocket. Cut one 8″ × 9″
pocket piece from the terry cloth. Overcast
one 9″ edge. Fold the overcast edge toward
the right side of the fabric, forming a 1½″
top facing. Stitch the 2 layers together along
the raw edges, using a ½″ seam allowance. Trim the raw edges to ¼″ and turn
right side out. Hand-stitch the overcast
edges to the wrong side of the pocket.

Press under ½″ on the side and bottom
raw edges. Pin the wrong side of the pocket
to the right side of the wrap. Position it 9″
in from the striped edge and 9″ up from
the hem edge. Topstitch the side and bottom edges to the wrap, reinforcing the 2
top corners with a triangle of stitching.

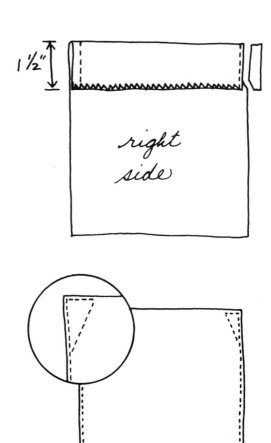

►**HINT.** Make this bathwrap up in
school or team colors. Add the school
emblem or the player's numbers to the
front, instead of initials.

Silky Aviator's Scarf with Satin Stitch Monogram

MATERIALS:

1½ yards 36"- or 45"-wide white silk or synthetic fabric
1 skein 6-strand embroidery floss to match the fabric
Letter monogram transfer or pattern
White thread

DIRECTIONS:

Cutting. Trim ½ " of fabric off evenly along one selvage edge. Measuring on the cross grain, mark a point 29 " from this cut edge. Continue marking this 29 "-width along the entire length of the fabric. Connect the marks by drawing a line. Cut on the line.

Straighten one 29 " edge of the piece by pulling a thread and cutting along the pulled thread. Measure 52 " from this end to the opposite end and pull a thread at that point. Cut along the pulled thread as before.

Fringe. Carefully fringe the fabric along one 29 " edge. Pull off 1 or 2 threads at a time until you have a 1 "-deep fringe. To prevent unraveling, machine straight stitch across the base thread of the fringe, using 10 to 12 stitches per inch. Repeat this on the opposite 29 " edge.

Assembly. With right sides together, fold the fringed scarf piece in half lengthwise to form a tube. Match the long raw edges and pin them together. Match the fringed ends. Machine-stitch the raw edges together, using a ½ " seam allowance. Trim the seam allowance evenly to ¼ " and overcast the raw edges together.

Turn the scarf right side out through one end. Press the scarf flat along the seam line. Smooth the scarf out flat and crease it in half along the opposite edge.

Monogram. At one end of the completed scarf, fold it in half lengthwise, matching the seamed edge to the folded edge. Crease lightly with your iron. Open out flat.

Fold the same end of the scarf up evenly 4 " (including fringe). Crease lightly as before. Baste through only one layer of fabric, along both crease lines, to mark the monogram placement.

Transfer the monogram to one side of the scarf, centered over the basting lines. Use a hand satin stitch to embroider the monogram. Refer to Hand-Embroidered Monograms in Chapter 1. Work the monogram through one thickness of fabric, so the wrong side will not be visible when it is worn.

►HINT. This scarf will be a hit in any neutral color. Make it in beige, brown, gray, or black for the man on your best-dressed list. The monogram should always match the fabric for a subtle, sophisticated look.

Two-tone Heather Wool Scarf

MATERIALS:

½ yard 54″-wide light-colored heather wool (lightweight)
¼ yard 54″-wide dark-colored heather wool (lightweight)
2″ letter transfers or Gothic stencils
Thread to match both fabrics

DIRECTIONS:

Cutting. It is important to use the pulled thread method of cutting, as described under the Silky Aviator's Scarf. Cut one 15″ × 35″ scarf and two 3″ × 15″ borders from the light-colored wool. From the dark- colored wool, cut two 3″ × 15″ borders and two 8″ × 15″ end pieces.

Letters. Follow the Machine-Appliquéd Letters instructions in Chapter 1 to stitch the letters to one end piece of the scarf. Cut the letter from the light-colored wool. Position it 2½″ up from one 15″ edge and 2½″ in from the 8″ edge on the right-hand side.

Borders. Stitch one 3″ × 15″ dark border to each end of the 15″ × 35″ scarf piece. Use a flat-fell seam. With the wrong sides together, match one 15″ edge of each piece. Pin and stitch the seam, using a ½″ seam allowance. Trim the light-colored seam allowance to ¼″. Press under ¼″ on the dark-colored seam allowance. Press it toward the light-colored side and pin it flat. Edgestitch, using the dark thread on top and the light thread in the bobbin. Illustration at top.

Seam one 3″ × 15″ light-colored border to each dark border at both ends of the scarf. Use the flat-fell seam, following previous instructions. Repeat this method to attach one 8″ × 15″ end piece to each end of the scarf. Illustration at bottom.

Fringe. Follow the fringing instructions under the Silky Aviator's Scarf to fringe both 15″ wide ends of the scarf.

Hems. Press ¼″ to the wrong side on each long side edge of the scarf. Press under ¼″ again, forming a narrow hem. Edgestitch the hem in place. Use light thread to stitch all the light-colored fabric areas. Change to dark thread to stitch the dark fabric areas. Secure all the thread ends neatly.

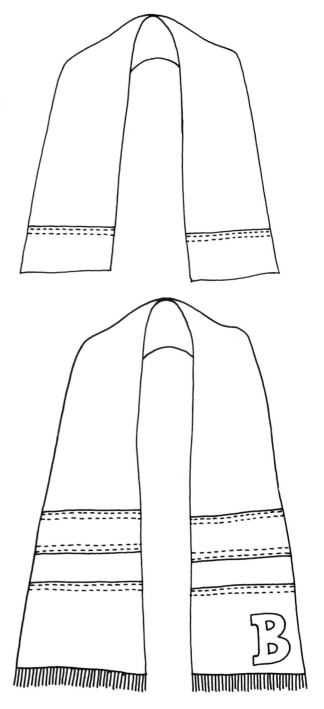

► HINT. Stitch this scarf up in 2 colors of satin to make a flashy splash for the sportsman or rock musician in your life.

Two-Color Status Scarf

MATERIALS:
½ yard 54″-wide lightweight green wool
¼ yard 54″-wide lightweight burgundy wool
1 skein burgundy 6-strand embroidery floss
Letter monogram or transfer
Burgundy and green thread

DIRECTIONS:

Cutting. Be sure to use the pulled thread method of cutting described under the Silky Aviator's Scarf. Trim off the fabric selvage on both sides. Cut two 6″ × 53″ green strips and one 7″ × 53″ burgundy strip.

Assembly. Fringe each short end of all the strips, following the instructions under the Silky Aviator's Scarf. Seam one green strip to each side of the burgundy strip. Use a flat-fell seam, following the instructions under the Two-tone Wool Scarf. Trim the burgundy seam allowances to ¼″ and press the green seam allowances on top. Match all the fringed ends carefully so they are even.

Letters. Apply the initials to the center burgundy stripe as indicated under the Silky Aviator's Scarf.

► Hɪɴᴛ. Try using up the remnants of wool tweeds that are left over from making classic slacks and jackets. Coordinate 2 or 3 strips of subtle fabrics for a well-tailored effect. Remember that all fabrics should be about the same weight, and avoid any heavy, itchy fabrics.

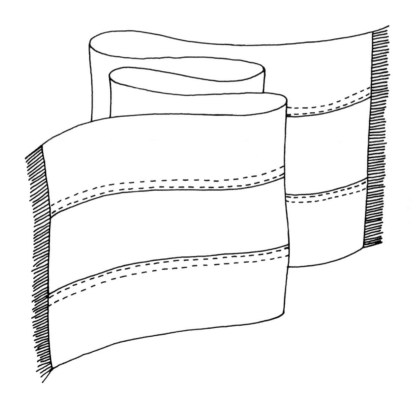

Father's Day Card Made of Sandpaper Patchwork

MATERIALS:

1 small package of assorted colors and grades of sandpaper
Off-white drawing paper
½" metallic gold paper stick-on letters
5½" × 8" envelope (or any large envelope)
Stick glue

DIRECTIONS:

Cutting. Measure the envelope and subtract ¼" from the length and width. The shorter dimension will become the card height. The longer dimension will become the card width. Draw a rectangle on the paper that measures 2 times the card height × the card width. Cut it out. Illustration A. Fold the card in half so it is held horizontally. Illustration B.

Patchwork design. Trace the triangle and square patterns onto cardboard and cut them out. Illustration C. Cut out the following pieces from the different sandpapers:

Light color: 4 squares, 12 triangles
Medium color: 4 squares, 4 triangles
Dark color: 12 triangles

Transfer the patchwork design to the card front. Center it so an even amount of the card front extends on all sides. Follow the layout guide to position the sandpaper pieces on the card. Glue each piece in place, weight it down, and allow it to dry thoroughly.

Lettering. Center the word "Dad" on the front cover with the stick-on letters. Refer to Chapter 1 for details on lettering. On the inside message area of the card, spell out "An Extra Fine Grade Father!" Either hand write it or draw baselines and spell it out with the stick-on letters. Spell it out in 3 lines. "An" is placed on the first line, "Extra Fine Grade" is on the second line, and "Father" goes on the third line.

► HINT. Use this card to send a get-well wish. Change the inside message to "Just the Card to Help You Smooth Over the Rough Edges!"

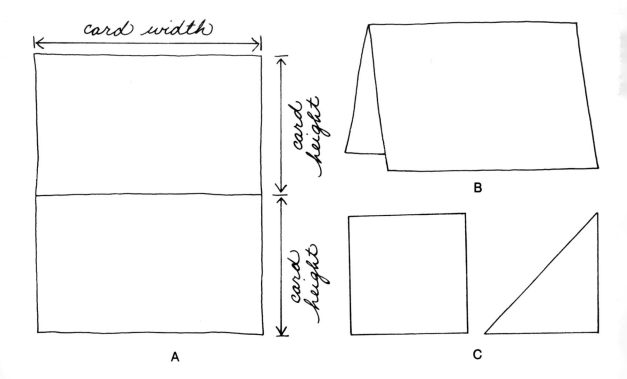

card width

card height

card height

A

B

C

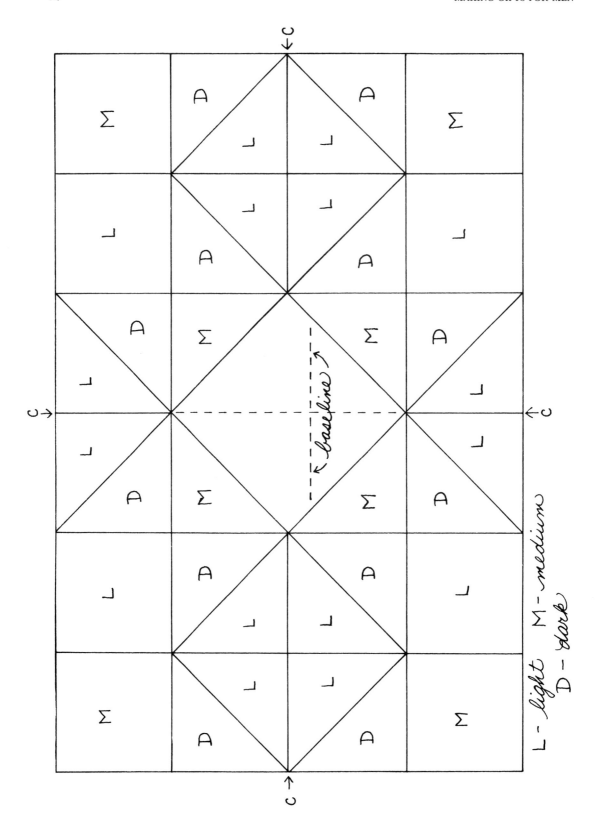

Happy Birthday Card with Paper Cutwork

MATERIALS:

Gray drawing paper
½ ″ black plastic stick-on letters
Striped decorative paper
5½ ″ × 8 ″ envelope (or any large envelope)
White glue

DIRECTIONS:

Cutting. Measure the size of the envelope. Subtract ¼" from the length and width dimensions. The longer dimension will become the card height. The shorter dimension is the card width. Draw a rectangle on the paper that measures 2 times the card width × the card height. Cut it out. Fold the card in half so it is held vertically.

Lettering. Mark the horizontal and vertical centers on the card front with lightly drawn lines. Draw a baseline for the letters ⅛" above and parallel to the horizontal center line. In the same manner, draw a line ⅝" below the center line. Letter "Happy Birthday" on the baselines, using the plastic letters. Center the letters on the vertical center line, referring to Chapter 1 for specific instructions.

Tie Cutouts. Trace the pattern onto a 4" × 6" piece of cardboard. Carefully cut out each tie, using a paper knife. Note that there is a ⅛" paper bridge between the tie and the knot of the tie. On the front of the card, draw a line 1" above and below the horizontal center line. Use the cardboard stencil to draw 5 ties on each line. Center the middle tie on the vertical center line. Carefully cut out each tie and knot, using a sharp paper knife.

Open the card out flat. Working over a thick layer of newspaper, cut out each tie with a paper knife. Cut two 3¼"-wide pieces of striped paper that are equal to the card width in length. Cut them so the stripes are placed diagonally. Glue the paper to the inside of the card where the message normally appears. Place them so the stripe design shows through the tie cutouts. Weight the card down and allow it to dry flat.

Message. Draw a baseline for the letters 1¼" below the upper piece of striped paper. Center the letters for "Tie-dings" on the baseline and press them in place as you did before.

▶ HINT.   Sew up a tie as a gift to accompany the card and glue a swatch of the actual tie fabric inside the card instead of paper.

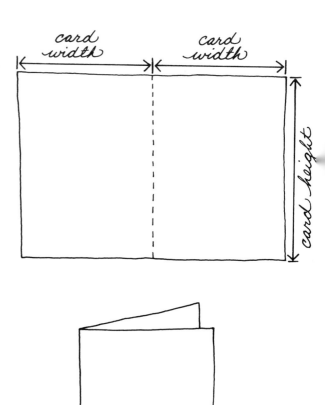

I Love You Card Using a Collage of Letters

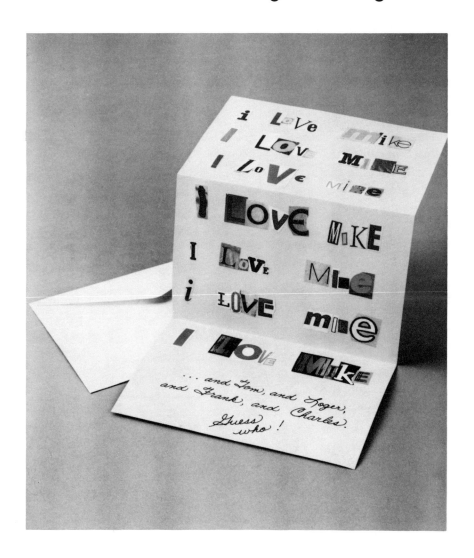

MATERIALS:

Yellow drawing paper
Assorted magazines for cutout letters
5½ ″ × 8 ″ envelope (or any large envelope)
Stick glue

DIRECTIONS:

Cutting. Measure the envelope and subtract ¼" from the length and width. The shorter dimension will become the card height. The longer dimension will become the card width. Draw a rectangle on the paper that measures 3 times the card height × the card width. Cut it out. Lightly draw 2 fold lines across the card width on the right side of the paper. Space them the card height measurement apart, so that you are dividing the card into thirds. Fold one fold line in one direction and the other in the opposite direction, accordion style.

Letters. Cut out enough magazine letters to spell "I Love [insert name]" 7 times. Choose fancy, decorative letters in bright colors. The message is repeated 3 times on each of the top 2 folded sections of the front of the card. Place the letters in 3 lines, spacing them as needed to fit. Repeat the message one more time on the top of the third section.

Pick up one letter at a time. Apply stick glue to the wrong side and press it back in place. Repeat this with each line until the 7 lines are complete.

Message. On the very bottom edge of the card, use your own handwriting to say ". . . and Tom, and Roger, and Frank, and Charles!"

▶ HINT. This is a great idea for kids who want to make their own cards for Dad. It's really simple and lots of fun. It will keep them busy for hours, spelling out their *own* messages and searching for the right letters.

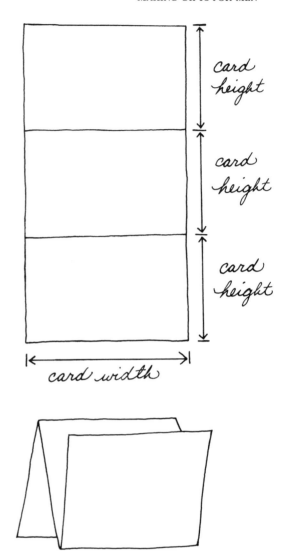

3.

Make It to Take Along

PROJECT

Roll-up Tool Kit for the Car

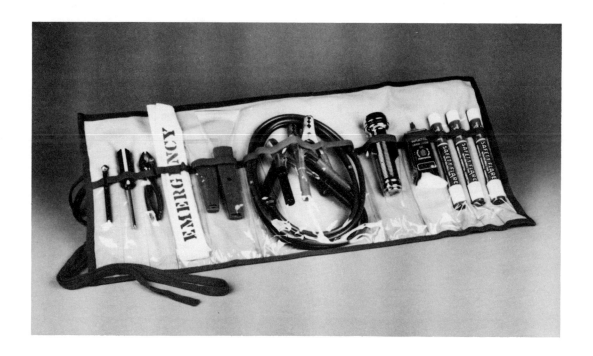

MATERIALS:

1⅛ yard 44"-wide gray canvas
⅜ yard 52"-wide heavyweight clear plastic
9 yards 1¼"-wide red twill tape or grosgrain ribbon
Gray and red thread
Black china marker or grease pencil
Suggested kit ingredients: jumper cables, air gauge, flares, oil, pliers, screwdriver,
  wrenches, flashlight, ice scrapers, emergency handkerchief.

DIRECTIONS:

Cutting. Straighten the edges of the canvas and plastic before cutting. From the canvas, cut two 18″ × 37¼″ base pieces. Cut a plastic pocket 11″ × 49¼″.

Pocket. Small pleats are made in the bottom of the larger plastic pockets to allow room for inserting large items. The 2″ pockets have no pleats. The 3″ and 4″ pockets have ½″ pleats on each side. The 10″ pocket has a 1″ pleat on each side. Using the china marker, place marks along both long edges of the plastic pocket spaced at the following intervals:

⅝″ seam allowance
2″ pocket – 2″ pocket – 2″ pocket
1″ pleat – 3″ pocket – 1″ pleat
1″ pleat – 4″ pocket – 1″ pleat
2″ pleat – 10″ pocket – 2″ pleat
1″ pleat – 4″ pocket – 1″ pleat
1″ pleat – 3″ pocket – 1″ pleat
2″ pocket – 2″ pocket – 2″ pocket
⅝″ seam allowance.

Connect the corresponding marks on each edge with lines.

The 49¼″ top edge of the plastic pocket is bound with twill tape. Position the edge of the tape along the plastic edge so it overlaps ⅝″. Pin and topstitch in place (below) along the edge of the tape.

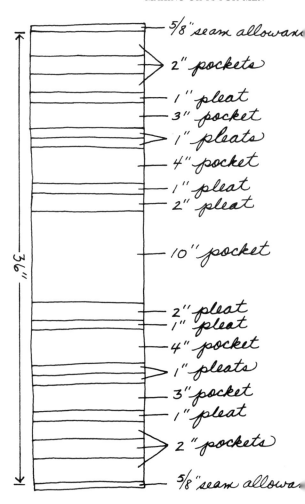

5/8" seam allowance
2" pockets
1" pleat
3" pocket
1" pleats
4" pocket
1" pleat
2" pleat
10" pocket
2" pleat
1" pleat
4" pocket
1" pleats
3" pocket
1" pleat
2" pockets
5/8" seam allowance

36"

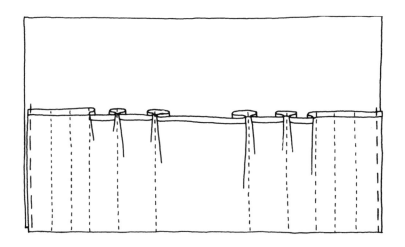

Note. Do not iron the plastic! Fold the tape in half over the edge of the plastic and topstitch this side in place in the same manner.

Put the pocket section on top of the right side of one of the base pieces. Baste the 11″ ends to the 18″ raw edges of the base piece so they are even with the bottom of the kit. The pockets are divided by rows of machine-stitching. Beginning at one end make 2 rows of stitches spaced $\frac{1}{16}$″ apart on top of the first 2″ pocket line. Begin at the bottom raw edge, stitch to the bound edge, turn, and stitch back to the raw edge. Repeat this on the next two 2″ pocket lines and on the 3 at the opposite end of the kit.

The remaining pockets have pleated bottoms. To make the pleats, fold the plastic along the pocket dividing line. Match the fold to the adjoining pocket edge at the bottom. Baste the pleat to the canvas $\frac{1}{4}$″ from the bottom edge. Make 2 pleats in the bottom of each of the remaining pockets in this manner. Straighten the pocket dividing lines so they are vertical. Pin them to the canvas and stitch as you did on the 2″ pockets.

Note. The presser foot may not glide smoothly over the plastic. Cut strips of tracing paper and hold them over the plastic during stitching. You can see the stitching lines through the tracing paper. Tear the paper away after the stitching is completed.

Assembly. Double the canvas base piece to support the heavy contents of the tool kit. With the wrong sides together, match the raw edges of the 2 base pieces. Pin and baste them together, using a $\frac{1}{4}$″ seam allowance.

Bind the top and bottom edges of the kit with twill tape as you did on the top of the pocket. The bottom edges of the pocket are encased with the tape.

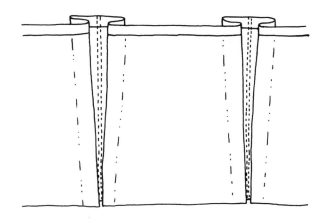

Ties. Cut two 18″ and two 36″ lengths of twill tape. Press under $\frac{1}{2}$″ on one end of each piece. Press the tape in half lengthwise, matching the long edges. Edge-stitch the ties and finished ends flat.

Place the pocket side of the tool kit down flat. Mark points on one 18″ end 5″ from the top and bottom edge. Baste the raw end of one long tie at each point. Baste one short tie on top of each long one.

Bind each 18″ edge of the kit with twill tape, encasing the tie ends. Finish the ends of the tape by folding $\frac{1}{2}$″ to the inside before stitching. Fill the kit pockets. Roll it up, beginning at the plain 18″ end. Wrap the long ties around the kit and tie to the shorter tie.

▶ **Hint.** This Tool Kit is ideal for holding almost any assortment of tools. The sizes of the pockets are easily customized to meet the needs of carpenters, gardeners, handymen, and just about every type of hobbyist. Simply enlarge or reduce the pocket sizes to accommodate the kinds of tools that are used.

Emergency Handkerchief to Stencil

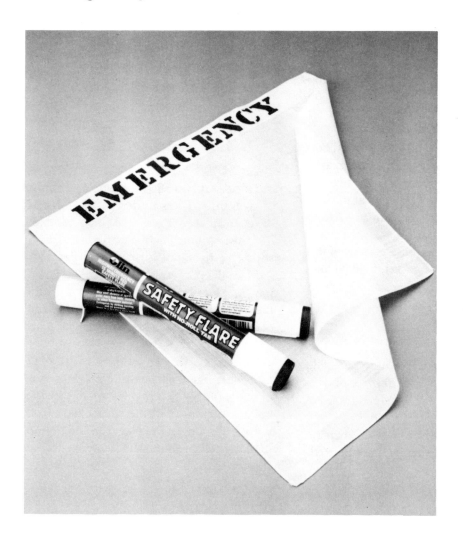

MATERIALS:

1 plain white handkerchief
1 ″ Roman letter stencils
Bright red acrylic paint in a small tube
Small stencil brush
White thread

DIRECTIONS:

Stenciling. On the right side, draw a baseline for the letters 2¾" from and parallel to one edge of the handkerchief. Outline the stencil letters lightly in pencil. Begin with the middle *g,* and work to the left and right, placing letters as described in Chapter 1.

Tape the handkerchief to newspaper so it is held flat. Stencil the letters as described under the Beach Chair in Chapter 7.

Casing. A 1½" casing is made on the lettered side of the handkerchief to slip over the car aerial in the event of an emergency. Press 1½" of the handkerchief to the wrong side. Pin closed the edge and across the end of the casing at the end of the word "Emergency." The closed casing end holds the handkerchief at the top of the aerial. Edgestitch the casing as pinned.

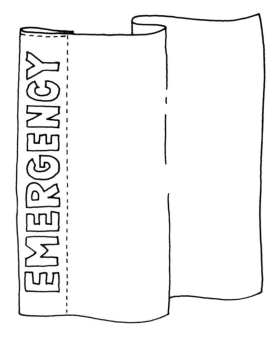

► **HINT.** Men's handkerchieves make perfect instant cloth napkins. Pick out some with a plaid border, omit the casing, and stencil your favorite gourmet's name or initials on them just as described for the Emergency Handkerchief.

Thermos Carrier Sewn with Quilted Nylon

MATERIALS:

One thermos approximately 13½" tall with a circumference of
no more than 12"
½ yard red prequilted nylon
½ yard 1"-wide red nylon webbing
⅞ yard ¼" cotton cord
One yard 2"-wide red bias tape
12" zipper
Red thread

DIRECTIONS:

Cutting. From the quilted fabric, cut one 11″ × 14″ carrier bottom, one 4″ × 14″ carrier top, and two 5″ circles.

Zipper. The zipper is inserted between the top and bottom of the carrier. With the right side of the bottom against the right side of the zipper, match the edge of the zipper tape to one 14″ edge. Place the ends of the zipper tape even with one end of the fabric, so the zipper stop is about ¾″ from the fabric edge. Baste the zipper in place so 1¼″ of fabric extends beyond the top of the zipper teeth. Machine-stitch using a ¼″ seam allowance and overcast the raw edges. Repeat this with the carrier top on the other side of the zipper.

Webbing. Stitch the seam closed above the top of the zipper, using a ¼″ seam allowance. Clip the seam allowances at the top of the zipper tape so the seam lies flat. Cut a 15½″ piece of webbing. Match one end of the webbing to the top edge of the carrier. Leave a ⅝″ seam allowance to the right of the webbing. Pin the webbing to the carrier for a distance of 5½″. Machine edgestitch in place. Edgestitch up from the raw edge, stitch across the webbing at the 5½″ mark, and edgestitch back to the raw edge. Make a 1″ boxed X of stitching for extra strength on top of the edgestitching at the 5½″ mark. Repeat this on the bottom, stitching up 4½″. The 5½″ arched handle is automatically formed between the boxes of stitching by the extra length of webbing.

Assembly. With right sides together, match the two 14″ edges along the handle side. Machine-stitch using a ½″ seam allowance. Overcast all raw edges. Make sure the handle doesn't get caught in the seam.

Make piping from the cotton cord and bias tape as described under the Zippered Binder in Chapter 3. Apply the piping

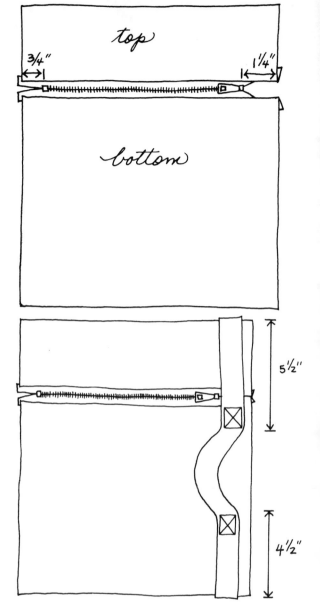

around each 5″ circle, using a ½″ seam allowance. Finish the ends neatly where they meet. Tuck under one raw end of the bias tape. Trim the cord to fit and baste the seam allowances flat to the circle.

With right sides together, baste one circle to one end of the carrier. Machine-stitch, trim the seam allowance to ¼″, and overcast the raw edges. Repeat on the other end. Turn the carrier right side out through the zipper opening and insert the thermos.

▶ **HINT.** Make this carrier in canvas to be used as a lightweight mini-tool kit for the car.

Stadium Blanket to Crochet

MATERIALS:

Seven 3½-ounce skeins 4-ply yarn in the lighter school color
1 yard 54″ heavy blanket wool fabric in the darker school color
8 school emblems
½ yard fabric fuser
Size F crochet hook
Large-eyed embroidery needle

DIRECTIONS:

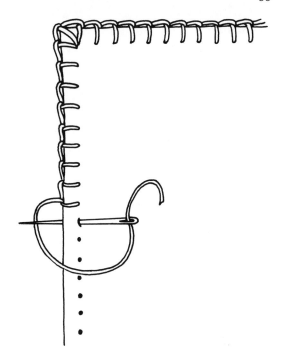

Fabric Squares. Cut eight 12″ × 12″ squares from the wool fabric. The raw edges of each square are finished with a buttonhole stitch. Overcast the raw edges of the squares in matching thread if the fabric unravels very badly. Place chalk dots every ¼″ along the 4 raw edges of the wool square. Place the dots ¼″ in from the raw edge. There are 49 stitches on each side. Using the yarn, work a buttonhole stitch at each mark. Make 3 buttonhole stitches at each corner dot to turn the corner. Knot and secure the end of the yarn and sink it into the stitches invisibly.

Each emblem is backed with fabric fuser so it can be ironed on to the wool squares. Pin the emblems to the fabric fuser. Cut the fuser so it is exactly the same shape as the emblem. Center one emblem on the right side of one wool square. Remove the pins. Cover with a terry towel and steam, following the manufacturer's instructions. Allow each one to cool before moving them.

Crochet squares. Make eight 12″ × 12″ crocheted squares as follows:

Gauge: 4 dc = 1″   2 rows = 1″

With the yarn, ch 48 plus 3 to turn (51 sts).

Row 1: insert the hook in the 4th ch from hk, work 1 dc in each ch across, ch 3, turn (48 sts).

Rows 2 to 23: insert the hook into the 2nd st from the hook, work 1 dc in each st across, ch 3, turn.

Row 24: repeat row 2, knot end, and sink yarn end into stitches invisibly. Block each square to 12″ × 12″, following the manufacturer's instructions.

Assembly. The Stadium Blanket is made up of 4 rows of 4 squares each. Lay the fabric and crocheted squares out on the floor in a checkerboard manner. Begin with a fabric square, and alternate fabric and crocheted squares. Make sure all the emblems are held upright. Place all the crocheted squares so the crocheted rows are held horizontally.

The squares are joined by slip stitches made from the *wrong* side. First, join the squares into 4 rows. Match the sides of one fabric square and one crocheted square. With yarn, work slip stitches through the corresponding stitches on each edge. One slip stitch is made into each buttonhole stitch on the fabric square. On the side edges of the crocheted square, 2 slip stitches are inserted into each double crochet.

The rows are joined together in the same manner. Work slip stitches into each buttonhole stitch and each double crochet stitch. Work one stitch into the seams between the squares. Tie off all yarn ends neatly. Lightly steam all of the crocheted seams flat. Add fringe to the top and bottom of the blanket following the directions given for the Simple Scarf.

► **HINT.** Use up your old blankets to make a great patchwork afghan. Cut squares from assorted colors of blankets that go together. Crochet them together with black or a neutral color of yarn, omitting the crocheted squares and emblems.

Zippered Binder with Western-Style Stitching

MATERIALS:

One 3-ring notebook approximately 12″H × 10½″W × 2″D
1 yard 44″-wide brown imitation suede
2¼ yards ¼″ cotton cord
Two 20″ heavy-duty zippers
Brown thread
Heavy topstitching thread in bright yellow, orange, and red

DIRECTIONS:

Pattern. Open the notebook out flat on
a large piece of paper. Draw around the entire outer edge. Mark the placement of the
spine fold lines by drawing lines on the pattern. Remove the notebook and add ¾" to
all outside edges for ease and seam allowances. Cut the pattern out.

One quarter of the stitching design is
given in the illustration. Cut a 10½" ×
10½" piece of plain white paper. Fold it
into quarters, crease the folds, and open it
out flat. Transfer the design to each quarter
of the paper, matching the centers as
indicated.

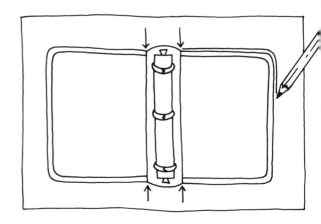

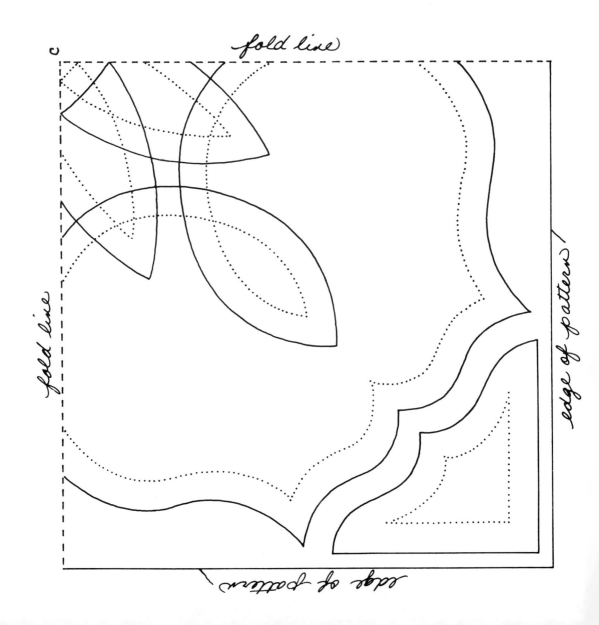

fold line

c

fold line

edge of pattern

edge of pattern

Cutting. Use the pattern to cut out one cover piece. Remove the pattern and cut one side of the paper pattern off along the spine fold line. Use this to cut 2 facing pieces. Cut 2 gusset pieces that measure 1½" × 41". Cut two 1¾" × 9" handle pieces.

Stitching design. Center the paper design on the *front* section of the suede cover piece. Baste the pattern to the suede. Baste an X across the design to prevent it from shifting during stitching. Set your machine to make 10 to 12 stitches per inch. With the red thread, carefully topstitch on all the solid lines of the design, turning and pivoting as needed. You will be stitching through the pattern and the suede at the same time. Pull all the thread ends to the back side and tie them securely.

Change to yellow thread and stitch all the dotted design lines in the same manner as you did for the red. Remove the paper pattern completely. Tear it along the stitching where it was perforated by the machine needle. Do not stitch any more rows through the paper because it becomes too difficult to remove.

Each channel of the design contains 6 rows of stitching, 2 red, 2 orange, and 2 yellow. Two rows of each color are placed together, spaced ¹⁄₁₆" apart. Work a second row of yellow inside the first. Change back to red and make a second row of red inside the first. Fill the channels by stitching 2 rows of orange, ¹⁄₁₆" apart, in the remaining space between the red and yellow rows.

Facings. The cover of the binder is held in place by facings. Hem one long edge of each facing piece by pressing ¼" to the wrong side. Machine-stitch this narrow hem in place. Baste the facing pieces to the cover, placing the wrong sides together. Position one facing on each side of the cover, matching outer raw edges on 3 sides. The narrow hems are directed toward the center.

Piping. For a professional look that lends support and provides strength and durability to edges that get lots of wear, make matching piping from the suede. Cut a bias strip of suede that measures 1½" × 77". If necessary, you may seam together small pieces to equal the length required. Fold the bias piece in half lengthwise over the cotton cord, placing the wrong sides together. Pin and stitch the raw edges together close to the cord, using a zipper foot on your machine.

Begin applying piping at the bottom edge of the back section of the cover. With right sides together, match the raw edges of the piping and the cover. Pin the piping around the entire outer edge of the cover. Clip the piping seam allowances at the corners so they will spread out flat and make a nice corner. Butt the ends of the piping together, trimming the cord to fit and overlapping the ends neatly.

Assembly. Slip the notebook into the cover and close it. On the seam allowance, mark the 4 spots where the spine folds. Remove the notebook. Make a ½" deep clip through the seam allowances at each mark. Use glue or a small scrap of fabric fuser to hold the clipped seam allowance flat to the wrong side.

The 2 zippers are joined so that the bag can be unzipped from the center. Pin the tops of the zipper tapes together so that the zipper pulls face each other. Sew the tops of the tapes together by machine about ¼" from the beginning of the zipper teeth. Press the seams open and hand-tack the free ends of the tape flat to the wrong side.

The zipper is inserted between the two gusset pieces. Mark the center of each gusset by folding it in half. With right sides together, place the tops of the joined zippers at the center mark on one gusset. Match the raw edge of the gusset to the edge of the zipper tape and machine-stitch.

Repeat this with the second gusset piece on the other side of the zipper tape.

The completed gusset is sewn to the cover. With right sides together, place the center of the gusset to the center point of the cover, in the middle of one short side. Baste the gusset to the cover. Do not cut off the extra length of gusset. Trim the seam allowances to ¼". Repeat on the other side of the gusset. Turn the cover right side out through the zipper opening.

Place the notebook in the cover. The extra length of zipper and gusset allows the notebook to open flat. Tuck each end of the gusset into the opening between the cover and the notebook.

► **HINT.** This project makes an ideal soft briefcase for writing materials or books. Omit the notebook and insert 2 pieces of heavy cardboard under the front and back facings.

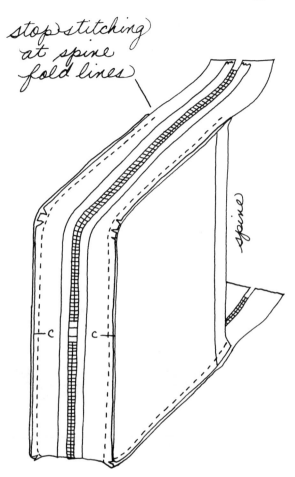

stop stitching at spine fold lines

Duffle Bags to Stitch in Four Sizes

MATERIALS:

44"-wide gray or silver quilted nylon
   small—1 yard, medium—1⅛ yards, large—1⅜ yards, extra-large—1⅝ yards
¾"-wide black twill tape or grosgrain ribbon
   small—2 yards, medium—2⅛ yards, large—2⅝ yards, extra-large—2¾ yards
2"-wide black nylon webbing
   small—3¾ yards, medium—4⅛ yards, large—4¾ yards,
   extra-large—5⅛ yards
1 black heavy-duty zipper
   small—16", medium—20", large—24", extra-large—28"
2 black heavy-duty zippers
   small—7", medium—7", large—9", extra-large—9"
Two 2" silver D-rings for each bag
Two 2" silver shoulder strap clips for each bag (optional)

DIRECTIONS:

Cutting. Directions are given for 4 sizes of bags:

small—16″L × 8″W × 8″H,
medium—20″L × 10″W × 10″H,
large—24″L × 12″W × 12″H,
extra-large—28″L × 14″W × 14″H.

Cut the following pieces from the quilted nylon:

1 bag body:
small—17″ × 29½″
medium—21″ × 37½″
large—25″ × 45½″
extra-large—29″ × 53½″
2 bag end pieces:
small—9″ × 9″
medium—11″ × 11″
large—13″ × 13″
extra-large—15″ × 15″
2 pockets:
small—8″W × 6½″H
medium—8″W × 8½″H
large—10″W × 10½″H
extra-large—10″W × 12½″H

Round the 4 corners of each end piece by drawing around a 3¼″ circle. Cut on the lines.

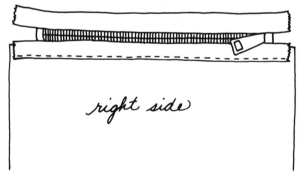

right side

Pockets. Overcast the 8″ (8″, 10″, 10″) top edge of each pocket piece. Position one of the short zippers on top of the overcast edge so it overlaps onto the pocket piece by ¼″. Straight stitch it in place. Center a piece of twill tape over this stitching line so it is ¼″ away from the zipper teeth. Cut the tape to fit. Edgestitch the tape to the zipper and the pocket. Repeat this on the other pocket piece.

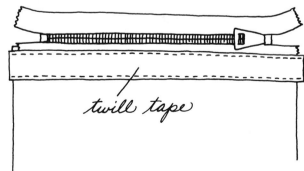

twill tape

With right sides together, pin the pocket pieces to the bag body. Center one pocket piece on the bag 10″ (13″, 16″, 19″) from each shorter end of the bag body. Machine-stitch across the pocket bottom. Flip the pocket over and edgestitch the top of the zipper tape to the bag. Center a piece of twill tape over the stitching and edgestitch it to the bag as you did before. The top edge of the tape is 4¼″ (5¼″, 6¼″, 7¼″) from and parallel to the edge of the bag. Baste the sides of the pockets flat to the bag body.

Handles. The handles are applied to the bag while it is flat and they are used to finish the side edges of the pockets. Cut a 87″ (99″, 117″, 130″) piece of webbing. Seam the short ends together, forming a ring. Make sure the webbing is not twisted. Press the seam allowance open.

Starting at the seam, fold the ring of webbing in half. Mark the fold with chalk. Working flat, mark the center of the bag body between the pocket bottoms. Pin the webbing seam, right side up, to the center mark. Position it so it straddles the raw edge of one side of each pocket. Baste the webbing to the bag body, starting at the zipper edge of one pocket and ending at the other.

Repeat this on the other side of the pockets, placing the chalk mark on the webbing at the center of the bag body. Edgestitch both sides of the webbing in place. Turn at the top of each pocket and stitch a 2½" boxed X on the webbing, as described under the Thermos Carrier.

The webbing is folded in half and stitched to form handles. Mark the center of each handle loop above each pocket. Make marks on each side 2½" away from the center mark. Fold the webbing in half toward the bag body, forming a 5" handle. Pin the woven edges together. Machine-stitch across the webbing at one mark, edgestitch the woven edges together, and stitch across at the other mark. Repeat on the other handle.

Zipper. Overcast both 17" (21", 25", 29") ends of the bag body. Topstitch the zipper to the overcast ends as you did on the pockets. You will have made the bag into a cylinder. Edgestitch twill tape over the zipper as you did before.

Optional Shoulder Straps. Cut two 2" lengths of webbing. Encase the straight side of each D-ring by folding the webbing in half through the ring. Baste the two raw edges of the webbing together.

Center the raw edges of the webbing over one end of the zipper. Pin and baste it in place. Repeat on the other end of the zipper.

Cut one 41" (43", 45", 47") piece of webbing for a shoulder strap. Press under ½" on each raw end. Insert one end through one shoulder strap clip as you did on the D-ring. Fold 3" of webbing to the wrong side. Topstitch a 2½" boxed X through both thicknesses as you did on the handles. Repeat on the other end, making sure both clips face the same direction.

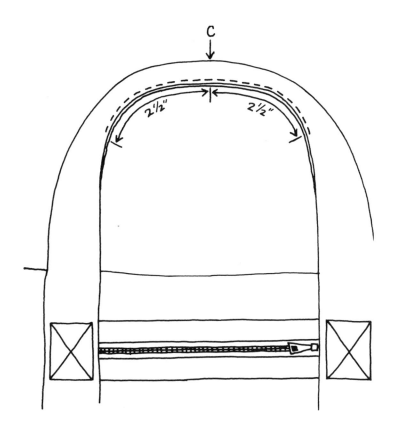

Assembly. Fold both open ends of the bag flat, matching the zipper to the center bottom mark of the bag. Make marks at the folds. Fold each end piece into quarters, marking each fold at the raw edge.

Turn the bag body inside out. With right sides together, pin one end piece to the open end of the bag. Match the 4 marks on the end piece to the zipper, center bottom, and 2 side marks on the bag body. Pin the end piece in place, easing in any fullness at the rounded corners. Open the zipper and repeat this on the other end. Trim the seam allowances to ¼" and overcast. Turn the bag right side out through the zipper.

► **HINT.** Use plain, unquilted nylon fabric to make these bags. They are perfect for stowing away all types of gear and they will pack absolutely flat when not in use.

Portable Spectator's Cushion

MATERIALS:

1 team emblem or logo (sew or iron-on)
1 yard 44"-wide fabric in a plain color that complements the team emblem
One 15" × 15" square of 2"-thick foam
3" × 10" piece of interfacing
Thread to match the fabric

DIRECTIONS:

Cutting. From the fabric, cut an 18 " × 35 " rectangle for the pillow cover. Cut a 14 " × 16 " pocket piece and a 3 " × 10 " handle and interfacing piece.

Handle. Baste the interfacing to the wrong side of the handle fabric, matching all raw edges. Press ½ " to the wrong side on both 3 " ends. Fold it in half lengthwise with the right sides together. Match the raw edges and the press-under ends. Stitch the raw edges together and trim the seam allowance to ¼ ".

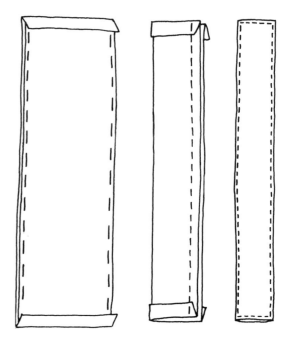

Turn the handle right side out and press it flat with the seam centered on one side. Edgestitch around the entire handle, closing the ends at the same time.

Fold the pillow cover in half, matching the 18 " ends. Crease and open out flat. Center the handle over the crease line on the right side of the fabric. Position it so that each end is 5 " in from each side edge. The handle will form an arch. Make a 1 " boxed X of stitching as described under the Thermos Carrier.

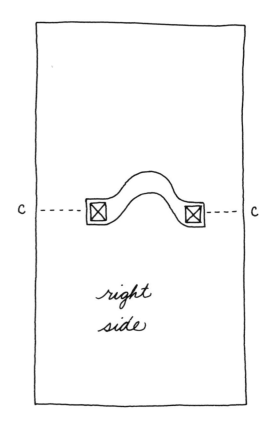

Program Pocket. Overcast one 14″ end of the pocket piece and make a 2″ facing at this end as described under the pocket instructions for the Terry Bathwrap in Chapter 2.

Press under ½″ on both side raw edges. Pin the wrong side of the pocket to the right side of the pillow cover. Position it so the bottom raw edge is centered on one 18″ end of the cover. The faced edge is toward the handle. Edgestitch the 2 sides of the pocket to the cover, reinforcing the 2 upper corners.

Assembly. With right sides together, fold the cover in half, matching the 18″ ends. The handle and pocket are inside. Match the side and bottom raw edges. Machine-stitch the sides and lower corners, leaving a 12″ opening centered on the bottom.

Each corner of the pillow cover is now darted to form a box pillow shape, as described under the Beach Chair pillow in Chapter 7.

Team emblem. If you are using an iron-on emblem, iron it directly onto the front of the carrier. Follow the manufacturer's instructions carefully. Sew-on emblems are stitched to the pillow front by hand or machine. Be sure to center it and place it upright so the handle is at the top side.

Put a sheet of plastic wrap around one edge of the foam pillow for easy inserting. Squeeze the sides of the foam inward, don't curl it, and insert it into the cover opening. Gently push it into each corner. Pull the plastic out and adjust if necessary. Tuck in the seam allowances and hand slip-stitch the opening closed.

▶ HINT. A good back cushion is something that everyone on your gift list would love. Use the design given in the Zippered Binder to make a decorated suede pillow front. Omit the pocket and the handle for a stay-at-home version.

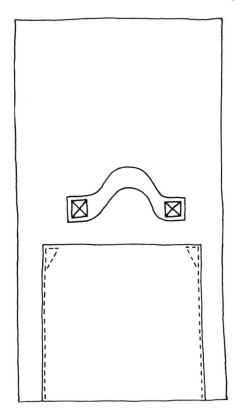

4.

Make It for Fun and Games

PROJECT
Chessboard Made with Ceramic Tiles

MATERIALS:
Thirty-two 2″ off-white ceramic tiles
Thirty-two 2″ brown ceramic tiles
Ceramic tile cement
16″ × 16″ square ¾″ plywood
6 feet flat 1″-wide decorative molding
Walnut wood stain
Wood glue

DIRECTIONS:

Tiles. The tiles are glued to the wooden base piece with tile cement. Separate the individual tiles out of the packaged sheets. Arrange them on the wood base in a checkerboard manner as described under the Checkerboard. Cement them to the base so they butt directly against each other, with no space in between the tiles. The playing surface should be absolutely flat, so use the cement sparingly. Allow them to dry, following the manufacturer's instructions.

Molding. Cut two 16" lengths of molding to finish the sides of the gameboard. Glue these to opposite ends of the plywood base so that the edges of the tile and the plywood are covered. Measure the two remaining sides of the base, including the molding. Cut two pieces to this measurement and glue them in place. Stain the molding, following the manufacturer's directions.

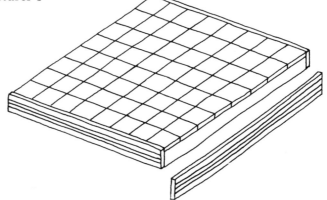

NOTE. The edges of the molding can be mitered to fit the base for a cleaner-looking corner. Have this done professionally when you purchase the lumber.

▶ HINT. Use tiles to cover the marred top of an old table. Set the chess/checkerboard into the center of the table and surround it with larger tiles. Finish the edge of the table with molding, as described for the gameboard base.

Chess Set to Assemble with Corks

MATERIALS:

Corks in 4 sizes—heights will vary propor-
tionately to the cork diameter
    52 extra-small #0 ($\frac{1}{4}$" diameter)
    10 small #2 ($\frac{1}{2}$" diameter)
    28 medium #4 ($\frac{3}{4}$" diameter)
    12 large #6 (1" diameter)
Hexagonal nuts in 4 sizes
    16 extra-small ($\frac{3}{8}$" diameter)
    8 small ($\frac{1}{2}$" diameter)
    32 medium ($\frac{3}{4}$" diameter)
    4 large (1" diameter)

NOTE. The cork and hexagonal nut
sizes given are approximate. Slight
variations in size will not change the
appearance of the set.

Brown fabric dye
Gold and silver enamel
Clear glue in a tube (for metal)
Clear high-gloss varnish or lacquer
Small arts and crafts brush

DIRECTIONS:

Corks. Perfectly shaped corks are rare. Use fine sandpaper to smooth any rough edges and flatten the ends of the corks so they will stand upright.

Half of the corks are dyed dark brown to make the darker chess pieces. The other half are left natural. Count out half of the corks in each size to be dyed dark brown—26 extra-small, 5 small, 14 medium, and 6 large. Place the fabric dye in a glass bowl and add 2 cups of hot water. Stir well and add half the corks. Allow them to soak for about an hour, stirring occasionally. The dark-brown corks must be a noticeably different color from the natural corks. Rinse the dyed corks until the water is clear. Allow them to dry thoroughly.

Hexagonal Nuts. Often hardware items like nuts have a coating of oil on them that prevents glue and paint from sticking. Fill a small bowl with soap and water. Wash all the nuts, rinse, and spread them out on a towel to dry completely.

Assembly. Each chess piece is different. Make an identical set of light pieces and dark pieces. Each set contains the following number of pieces:

1 king
1 queen
2 bishops
2 knights
2 castles
8 pawns

Follow the illustrations to assemble the chess pieces. Always begin with the bottom nut and work upward. Stack the parts on

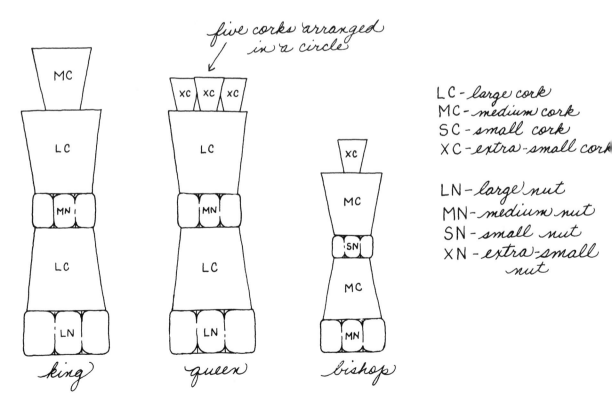

five corks arranged in a circle

LC - *large cork*
MC - *medium cork*
SC - *small cork*
XC - *extra-small cork*

LN - *large nut*
MN - *medium nut*
SN - *small nut*
XN - *extra-small nut*

king   *queen*   *bishop*

top of each other, centering them on the previous section. Spread the glue on each piece sparingly and press it in place. Hold it firmly in place for a few seconds before you continue.

Painting. The metal nuts are often discolored or scratched. Painting them with enamel gives them an even, attractive appearance. The nuts on the light chess pieces are painted silver and those on the dark pieces, gold. Use a small, pointed brush to carefully paint all the visible parts of the metal on each piece. Allow the paint to dry thoroughly, following the manufacturer's instructions.

Clear varnish or lacquer is applied to the completed chess pieces. This protects them from heavy wear and gives them a slick, glossy finish. Follow the manufacturer's instructions for applying 1 or 2 coats.

► **Hint.** Chess sets can be made with a wide assortment of small items. Collect unusual hardware, wooden shapes, or plastic parts to design your own chess pieces. You probably already have enough odds and ends around the house to get started. Use hexagonal nuts as described in the instructions to connect the parts. This gives them a nice weighted feel and makes all the pieces look uniform.

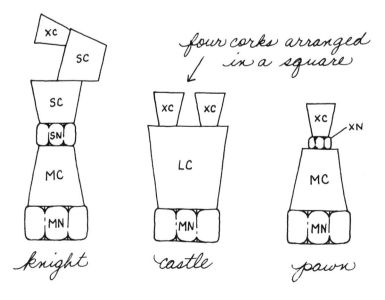

Checkerboard Anyone Can Make with Adhesive Paper

MATERIALS:

½ yard red flocked adhesive paper
¾ yard 18″-wide black adhesive paper
18″ × 18″ square of ¾″-thick wood for a base
6 feet flat decorative molding (¾″ wide)
Clear glue
Black paint
Grease pencil or china marker in a light color

DIRECTIONS:

Base. Cover the gameboard base with the black adhesive paper. Use the base as a pattern to draw and cut out a piece of black paper. Beginning at one edge, peel off the backing for about 2". Position the paper so it is even with the edge of the base. The side edges of the paper are also even with the sides of the base. Smooth the paper out, so it adheres to the base, removing any air bubbles as they occur. Pull the backing off gradually from underneath, smoothing the black paper down as you work. Check the side edges, keeping them even with the base. Cover the entire base and trim any excess paper off evenly with the edge. Burnish the paper with a soft cloth so it adheres well.

Red Squares. Use a grease pencil to outline the playing area of the board. Draw a line 2" in from and parallel to each side of the gameboard. Inside the playing area, draw a grid that has sixty-four 1¾" × 1¾" squares. You will be placing 8 squares across and 8 down.

On the backing side of the red flocked adhesive paper, draw thirty-two 1¾" × 1¾" squares. Cut them out with a paper knife.

Lay out the red squares inside the playing area on the board. Beginning at one corner, put a red square in every other space on the grid. Peel off the backing and match the edges of the red square to the drawn lines on the grid. Cover the entire playing area in this checkerboard manner, so that black and red squares are always next to each other. Remove any visible grease pencil marks with a tissue.

Molding. Molding is glued to the entire outer edge of the board. Cut two 18" pieces and glue them to opposite sides of the board. Measure the distance between the molding strips on the bare sides of the board. Cut 2 pieces to this measurement and glue them in place as before. Paint the molding and the edges of the base black.

NOTE. The corners of the molding can be mitered for a more professional finish. When you purchase the wood have the lumberyard or a carpenter cut these to fit the gameboard exactly.

► HINT. Use adhesive paper to center a checkerboard on the top of a card table. Make sure the surface is clean before positioning the adhesive paper. Proceed as just described, eliminating the base and the molding.

Checkers to Make from Corrugated Cardboard

MATERIALS:

20½″ × 20½″ sheet of one-sided corrugated cardboard (smooth paper is found
   on only one side)
Twenty-four 1⅜″-diameter washers
Black and red spray paint
White glue
Clear glue (for metal)

DIRECTIONS:

Cutting. A $\frac{1}{2}$"W × $20\frac{1}{2}$"L strip of cardboard is needed to make each checker. The ribs of the cardboard are lined up so they are parallel to the $\frac{1}{2}$" width. Draw 24 strips on the cardboard and cut them out with a paper knife or heavy scissors.

If one-sided corrugated cardboard is unavailable, get the two-sided type found on any large cardboard box. Use a sponge to moisten one side of the cardboard with water. Do not saturate it. Allow the dampened side to sit for a few minutes and gently peel off the wet side of the cardboard.

Assembly. Each cardboard strip is rolled and glued into a coiled circle to form a checker piece. Beginning at one $\frac{1}{2}$" end, fold $\frac{1}{4}$" toward the smooth side of the cardboard and secure it with white glue. Gently roll the cardboard toward the smooth side, placing a stream of glue on the paper as you work. Be careful not to crush the ridges of the cardboard as you roll it. Keep the top and bottom edges of the cardboard even as you roll it so that the checker will sit flat on the checkerboard and "kinged" pieces. Repeat this on the remaining strips of cardboard and allow them to dry thoroughly.

Use the clear glue to mount each checker on a $1\frac{3}{8}$" washer. Wash any oil off the washers before gluing. Spread glue on the washer and center a cardboard checker on top of it. Repeat this for all the pieces and allow them to dry thoroughly.

Painting. Spread 12 checkers out on several layers of newspaper. Spray paint them red, following the manufacturer's instructions. Spray thoroughly from all angles so that the interior surfaces of the cardboard ridges are completely covered. Allow them to dry. Spray paint the remaining 12 pieces black in the same manner.

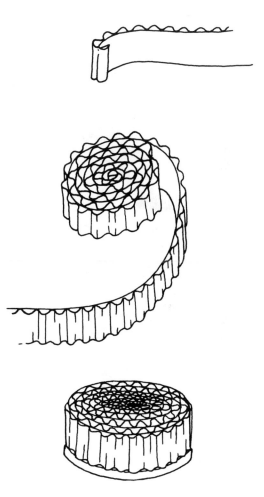

► HINT. These pieces can also be used as backgammon pieces. Make 15 game pieces in each color and use them with the Traveling Backgammon Board.

Traveling Backgammon Board Fused with Felt

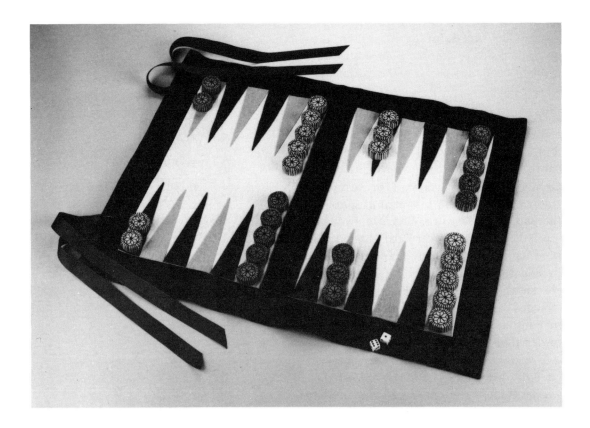

MATERIALS:

¾ yard brown felt
½ yard beige felt
Two 9″ × 12″ tan felt rectangles
Two 9″ × 12″ rust felt rectangles
1 yard fabric fuser
2 yards 1″-wide brown grosgrain
(See the project following for making the backgammon pieces.)

DIRECTIONS:

Cutting. Press the felt before cutting. Cut the following pieces from the felt:

Brown — One 20 " × 26 " base piece
Beige — One 16 " × 22 " gameboard
Brown — One 2 " × 16 " center bar

Use the triangle pattern to cut 12 pieces from the tan felt and 12 from the rust felt.

Assembly. The beige gameboard is centered on the brown base piece. Use the beige piece as a pattern to cut a piece of fabric fuser to the same size. Place the beige gameboard, backed with fuser, on the brown base so that the brown extends 2 " beyond the beige on all sides. Steam lightly, remove the pins, and then fuse the 2 pieces together, following the manufacturer's instructions.

Cut a piece of fuser to back the brown center bar. Position it across the middle of the gameboard so the ends match the edges of the beige felt and it is 10 " in from each end. Fuse it in place as you did before.

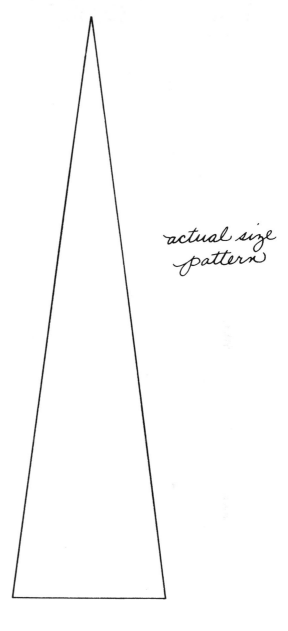

actual size pattern

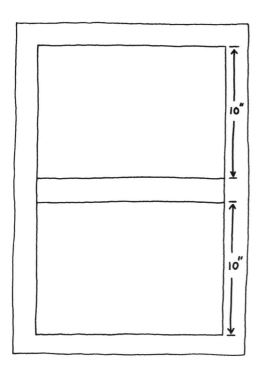

Back each triangle with fuser in the same manner. Pin 6 triangles in place along one 10 " side of the beige gameboard next to the center bar. Match the short flat end of the triangle to the edge of the beige felt. Make sure the triangle is upright and does not tilt left or right. Alternate tan and rust triangles. Repeat this on the other side of the center bar along the same side of the gameboard. Continue alternating the tan and rust triangles.

Twelve triangles are placed on the opposite side of the gameboard in the same manner. Alternate the colors of the triangles so that the different colors are facing each other on opposite sides of the gameboard.

Ties. Ties are fused to the back of the gameboard so it can be rolled up. Cut the grosgrain ribbon in half. Cut two 1 " × 1 " pieces of fuser. Fold one piece of ribbon in half. Pin the square of fuser at the halfway point of the ribbon. Position the center of the ribbon at the back of the gameboard 4 " in from the 26 " edge and 1 " away from the 20 " end. Repeat this with the other piece of ribbon on the other side of the gameboard. Roll the gameboard up from the plain end and tie the ribbon ties around it.

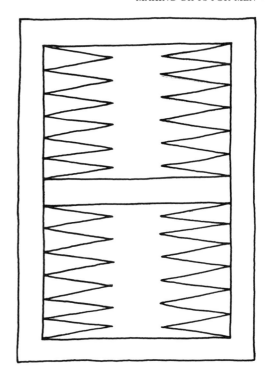

► **Hint.** Eliminate the ribbon ties and appliqué the felt gameboard to the center of a plastic tablecloth or card table cover. Use the directions for the Detachable Ball Carriers to make a case for storing the game pieces from the leftover felt.

Backgammon Pieces Decorated with Woodburning

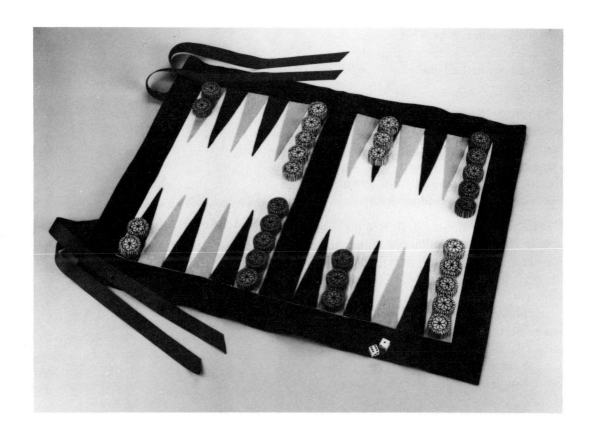

MATERIALS:

2 feet 1⅜" wooden dowel (closet pole)
Woodburning tool with a fine point
Gold and rust fabric dye
Clear varnish or lacquer

DIRECTIONS:

Sawing. The dowel is cut into ⅝"-thick "slices" to make 30 game pieces. The dowel can be cut with a hand-saw; however, it is time consuming and much less accurate than if it is cut professionally. I suggest that you have the lumberyard or someone experienced in carpentry cut it for you. Be sure to find out how much they will charge and also ask if they will sand the pieces for you. Sanding takes a long time and can be a bit messy. Having someone else do the cutting and sanding will cut in half the time needed to make the pieces.

Sanding. Each piece must be thoroughly sanded before being woodburned. Use coarse sandpaper to slightly round the cut edges on both sides. Finish the smoothing process with an extensive sanding, using fine sandpaper.

Pattern. Transfer the design to the top of each backgammon piece. Trace the design to paper and cut it out. Cut out an identical circle of carbon paper. Center the carbon on the top of one of the pieces with the carbon side against the wood. Put the pattern on top of the carbon and tape them both to the wooden piece. Using a ball point pen, go over the design lines. Press firmly but do not press too hard or you will make an indentation on the wood. Transfer the design to all the pieces in the same manner.

Woodburning. The woodburning tool is remarkably easy to use. The finer the point, the more exact your work will be. Be sure to keep safety in mind when using the tool and follow the manufacturer's instructions carefully. An inexpensive metal hot pad is ideal as a work surface. Be careful to avoid touching the heated parts of the tool. Use an old iron frying pan to hold the hot pen when you're not using it.

Test the tool on a piece of scrap wood before working on the backgammon pieces.

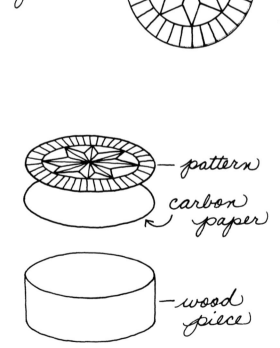

actual size pattern

— *pattern*

carbon paper

— *wood piece*

Try practicing both curved and straight lines. The woodburning technique should have a rustic look and it is not important to be extremely accurate. Each piece will naturally look slightly different.

When working on the top of the piece, position it flat on the work surface. Turn the wooden piece, rather than the tool, for the smoothest curved lines. Press firmly against the wood and always move the pen toward yourself. Take your time—the more slowly you work, the darker the lines will be.

Complete the woodburning design on the tops of all the pieces. The side of each piece is decorated with closely spaced straight lines like those you would find on the edge of a coin. The design line that begins on the top of the piece is simply continued down the side. Begin at the line on the top edge of the piece and draw a vertical line down the side of the piece with the tool. Repeat this with all the design lines around the edge of the piece. Complete the sides of all the pieces in this manner.

Finishing. The completed pieces are dyed gold or rust to indicate two different players. In a glass bowl, mix one package of gold dye with 3 cups of hot water. Dye 15 backgammon pieces gold. Soak them for about 10 minutes and then rinse them until the water runs clear. Allow them to dry thoroughly on a thick layer of newspaper. Repeat this with the rust dye on the remaining 15 pieces.

Use a small brush to apply clear varnish or lacquer to the top and sides of each piece. Follow the manufacturer's directions and allow them to dry completely before using them.

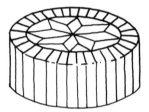

► **Hint.** For children or those who are not inclined to try woodburning, use a fine-point brown felt tip pen to draw the designs on the wood. Make sure the pen contains permanent ink that is not affected by water. This is an easy way to create a simulated woodburned look.

Racket Covers to Sew for Every Type of Racket

MATERIALS:

1 squash, racquetball, or tennis racket
½ yard of 44″-wide prequilted blue nylon
1 package ⅞″-wide white bias tape
1 heavy-duty white plastic zipper
   Length: squash—14″, racquetball—16″, tennis—18″
White thread

DIRECTIONS:

Pattern. Patterns are made by tracing around the head of the racket. Changes for each type of racket are given in parentheses. Working flat, draw a straight line down the center of your pattern paper. Center the head of the racket on this line so that exactly one half of the racket is positioned on either side of the line. Trace around the outer edge of the head of the racket. Do not trace around the handle. Remove the racket and draw a straight line across the section where the handle begins, connecting both sides of the racket outline. This line is the handle opening.

The outline of the racket should be a smooth, curved line. Working only on one half of the racket, correct the drawn lines to remove any bumps or irregularities that occurred due to the lacing of the strings. Fold the pattern along the center line. Trace the corrected shape onto the other half of the pattern. Add ¾" to all the outer edges of the pattern and cut it out.

Cutting. Use the pattern to cut 2 cover pieces from the quilted nylon. A gusset is placed between the cover pieces to allow for the thickness of the racket. The gusset length equals the zipper length plus 2½" (squash), 1½" (racquetball), or ½" (tennis). Cut one 1¼"-wide gusset piece to this measurement.

Optional Loop. For storing the racket, add a loop to the center of the top edge. Cut a 4" length of bias tape. With wrong sides together, fold it in half lengthwise, matching the 2 prefolded edges. Edgestitch the layers together.

Fold the bias tape in half, matching the raw ends and forming a loop. Baste the raw ends to one side of the cover at the center point of the top edge.

Binding. The handle openings are bound with bias tape first. Press the raw edge of one prefolded side of the bias tape

open. With right sides together, match the raw edges of the bias tape to the fabric raw edge. Pin them together along the bias crease line with a ¼" seam allowance. Machine-stitch the 2 layers together along the crease line.

Turn the fabric over and press the bias tape in half to the wrong side so it encases all the raw edges. The edge should overlap the previous row of machine-stitching by about ⅛". Baste it in place.

Working from the right side again, stitch in the "well" of the seam formed by the bias tape. The wrong side of the bias tape is secured and the stitching sinks into the seam so it is barely seen from the right side. Repeat this on the handle opening of the other cover piece and one short end of the gusset.

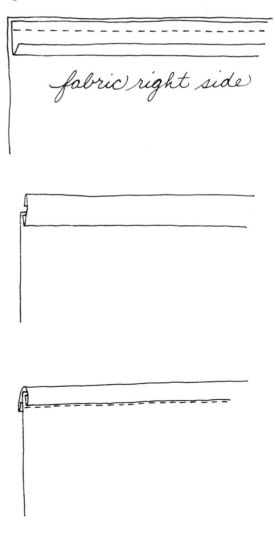

fabric right side

Zipper. The zipper is seamed to the gusset at the short unbound end. The zipper and the gusset should be the same width (1″–1¼″). If necessary, trim the gusset width so it matches the width of the zipper. With right sides together, match the bottom end of the zipper to the end of the gusset. Seam them together, press the seam toward the gusset, and tack it in place by hand. At the open end of the zipper just beyond the zipper stop, fold the excess zipper tape to the wrong side. Hand-tack the ends flat.

Assembly. Fold the completed gusset in half and mark the center points at each raw edge. With the wrong sides together, pin the completed gusset to one side of the cover. Match the center marks and ease in any excess fabric evenly around the curve. The short ends of the completed gusset should be even with the bound handle edges of the cover. Machine stitch the seam using a ¼″ seam allowance. Join the other side of the cover to the gusset in the same manner.

Bind the two curved seams of the racket cover with bias tape as just described. Begin applying the tape from the outside of the cover and press it in half toward the gusset. Finish the edges at the handle openings by pressing under ½″ before stitching.

► **HINT.** For a combination bag and racket cover, stitch one side of the completed racket cover to the side of the large Duffle Bag in Chapter 3. Center it and angle it on the bag so the handle of the racket is directed slightly upward.

Detachable Ball Carriers to Add to Any Racket Cover

MATERIALS:

3 squash, racquetball, or tennis balls
44"-wide prequilted blue nylon
   ¼ yard for squash
   ⅜ yard for racquetball or tennis
1"-wide white Velcro
   4" for squash
   6" for racquetball or tennis
½ yard ¼" white cord for a drawstring
Blue thread

DIRECTIONS:

Cutting. The Ball Carrier is designed to hold 3 squash, racquetball, or tennis balls. The changes for each size are given in parentheses. From the quilted nylon, cut a rectangle that measures 7″W × 7½″L for squash (racquetball—8½″W × 9½″L, tennis—10½″W × 11″L). Also cut one circle for the bottom of each bag: squash—3″ diameter (racquetball—3½″ diameter, tennis—4″ diameter).

Velcro. The ball carriers are to be made for the previous project, Racket Covers; however, they can be added to any racket cover or bag. Velcro holds the carrier in place, keeping the balls stored with the racket. Pull the hooked and fuzzy sides of the Velcro apart.

Open the racket cover as far as possible. Fold it in half from the top to the bottom. On the right side draw a chalk line on the fold line. Center the fuzzy side of the Velcro on the chalk line, spacing it evenly from the top and bottom of the racket cover. The wrong side of the Velcro is placed against the right side of the cover. Pin and edgestitch it in place, being careful to stitch through only one side of the cover.

The hooked side of the Velcro is stitched to the ball carrier in the same manner. Position it 1″ away from and parallel to the longer, 7½″ (9½″, 11″), side of the carrier piece. The end of the Velcro is 1″ up from the bottom edge of the carrier.

Assembly. With right sides together, fold the carrier piece in half, matching the 7½″ (9½″, 11″) edges. Stitch the seam, leaving a ½″ drawstring opening at a point ¾″ from the top edge of the carrier. Press the seam open.

The circular bottom is attached to the carrier next. Divide the bottom edge of the carrier in half by folding it flat at the seam. Mark the fold line at the raw edge. Match the seam to the mark, fold and mark as

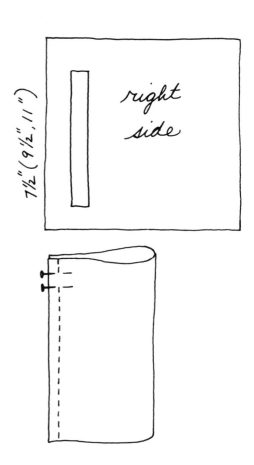

before, dividing the edge into quarters.
Fold the circular bottom piece into fourths
and mark the folds.

With right sides together, pin the circular
bottom to the carrier, matching the marks.
Ease in any fullness around the curve between the marks. Stitch and trim the seam
allowance to ¼". Overcast the raw edges
and turn the bag right side out.

Casing. The top of the bag is pulled
closed by the drawstring. To make a casing, overcast the top raw edge and press
¾" to the wrong side of the bag. Stitch the
casing in place ½" from the folded edge.

Insert a safety pin into one end of the
cording. Thread it through the casing,
entering and exiting at the ½" opening in
the seam. Knot each end of the cording and
tie in a bow to close the top of the carrier.

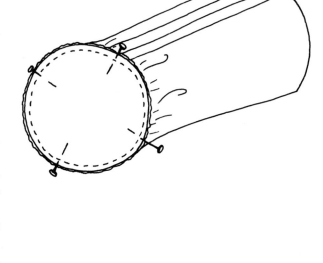

►**Hint.** This design makes a perfect
marble bag for your favorite young
troubleshooter! Make up the tennis ball
version in a soft fabric such as satin and
appliqué or embroider the word "Marbles"
on the side of the bag.

Golf Club Covers to Crochet and Cross-stitch

MATERIALS: (for 5 covers)

Three 3½-ounce skeins light yellow 4-ply yarn
Three 3½-ounce skeins dark green 4-ply yarn
Size F crochet hook

DIRECTIONS:

Covers. A set of 4 or 5 golf club covers is used for covering the woods in an average set of clubs. The crocheted covers can be made with a yellow or green stripe in the middle. The cross-stitch number is worked on the middle stripe in the opposite color. The instructions are the same for both color versions. Color A indicates the top and bottom stripes. Color B is the middle stripe.

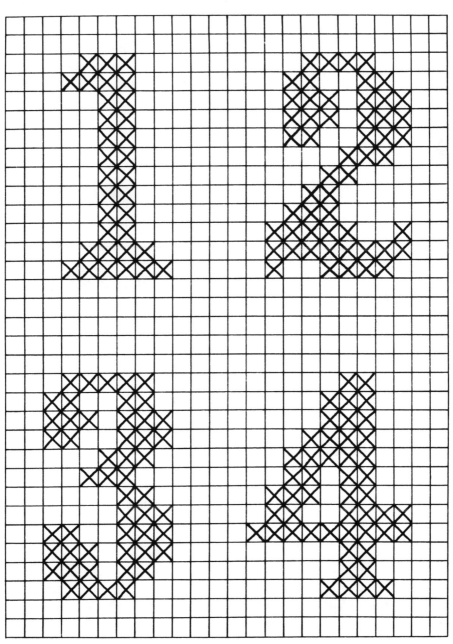

Gauge: 4 sc = 1″   4 rows = 1″

With color A yarn, ch 42 plus one to turn (43 sts)

Row 1: Insert the hook in the 2nd ch from hk, work 1 sc in each ch across, ch 1 turn (42 sts).

Rows 2–16: Insert the hook into the first stitch, work 1 sc in each st across, ch 1, turn (42 sts).

Rows 17–32: Change to color B. Insert the hook into the first stitch, work 1 sc in each st across, ch 1, turn (42 sts).

Rows 33–47: Change back to color A. Insert the hook into the first stitch, work 1 sc in each st across, ch 1, turn (42 sts).

Row 48: Insert the hook into the first stitch, work 1 sc in each st across, fasten off (42 sts).

Numbers. The club numbers are cross-stitched in the center of the middle stripe. Fold the crocheted piece in half and mark the center point on the middle stripe with basting stitches. With the opposite color, work one cross-stitch over each single crochet stitch. Use the charts to make each number. Position the number so it is 3 rows away from the top and bottom of the middle stripe.

Finishing. Block the crocheted piece to 10″W × 12″L. Join the two 12″ sides together with slip stitches made from the wrong side. Match the middle stripe at the seam. With matching yarn, work slip stitches through the corresponding stitches on each side. Steam the completed seam lightly. Tie off all yarn ends neatly.

The top end of the cover is gathered closed. With yarn and a large-eyed needle, pick up every other stitch around the top edge. Pull the yarn up tightly and tie the ends securely.

The gathered top of the cover is decorated with a large pom-pom. Use a paperback book to wind yarn for the pom-pom. Wrap the yellow yarn around the book crosswise 125 times. Cut a 10″ length of yarn and tie all the loops tightly together at their centers. Slip the yarn loops off of the book carefully. Insert the point of your scissors into each loop and cut it so all the yarn ends are approximately the same length. Make a green tassel in the same manner. Tie the center of the 2 tassels together and trim the ends evenly to form a nice ball-shape pom-pom. Sew the center of the pom-pom to the gathered top of the cover.

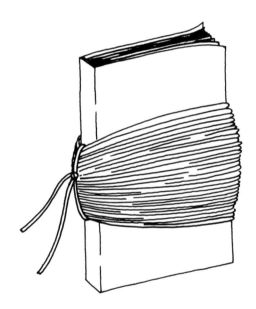

► **Hint.**   If you love to crochet but don't know any golfers, use these instructions to make a single crocheted scarf. Simply follow the same crochet directions, working 16 rows of each color alternately. Crochet 13 stripes of color, beginning and ending with the same color. Block the scarf to 10½″W × 52″L and add a fringe as described under the Simple Scarf in Chapter 5.

Light-Reflective Vest for Joggers and Bikers

MATERIALS:

1 yard red nylon
4½ yards ½"-wide light-reflective tape or ribbon (1⅞ yards yellow and 2¾ yards white)
6 yards ⅞"-wide yellow bias tape
Scraps of yellow fabric for appliquéd letters
2" Gothic letter stencils
⅛ yard fabric fuser
Thread to match the bias tape

DIRECTIONS:

Pattern. Working flat, draw a 12″ ×
36″ rectangle on paper. Cut it out and fold
it into quarters. Open it out flat and draw
lines on top of the folds. The shorter line
is the shoulder line of the vest.

The neckline opening is drawn at the
center of the vest. Draw a 4½″ × 4½″
square in the center of the large rectangle.
On another piece of paper, draw a 4½″
circle. Cut the circle pattern in half.

Align the straight edge of each half-circle
to the straight edges of the neckline at the
front and back and draw around it. Cut the
neckline opening out. Round the 4 outer
corners of the vest using the 4½″ circle.
Use the pattern to cut the vest from fabric.

NOTE.   If the fabric is very lightweight,
cut 2 vest pieces. Baste the 2 pieces together
along the neckline and outer raw edges.
Use the double layer as one piece of fabric.

Trimming. The front and back of the
vest are trimmed with light-reflective tape.
Position 3 rows of tape at a point 2½″
above one bottom edge of the vest. The
rows of tape should run parallel to the bottom edge of the vest. The center piece of
tape can be a different color if desired.
Edgestitch the tape in place, using matching thread. Apply 3 rows of tape 9½″
above the bottom edge in the same manner. Repeat on the other side of the vest.

Letters. Cut out and appliqué the word
"jogger" or "biker" in the 5½″ space between the 2 rows of reflective tape. Follow
the instructions for Machine Appliquéd
Letters in Chapter 1. Draw a chalk baseline
for the letters 1¾″ above the lower 3 rows
of tape. Center the letters on the baseline.

Ties. Cut four 16″ lengths of bias tape
for the ties. Press under ½″ on one end of
each piece. Fold each bias tape piece in half

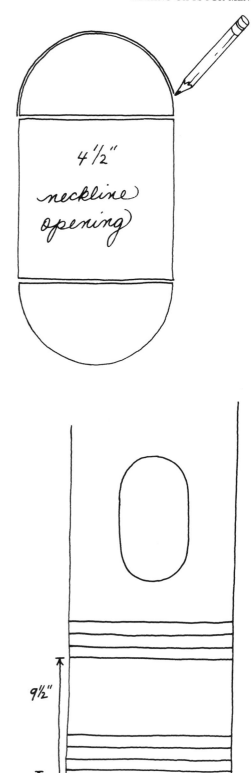

lengthwise and edgestitch the folded edges together. Repeat on the remaining 3 ties.

One tie is positioned on each side of the vest so it is even with the lowest stripe of reflective tape. On the wrong side of the vest, match the raw end of the tie to the edge of the vest so the raw edges are even. Baste each tie in place.

Binding. The neckline opening and outer edges of the vest are finished with bias tape. The raw ends of the ties are encased simultaneously with the binding. Follow the binding instructions given under the Racket Cover. Finish the ends of the bias by turning under ½ " where they meet.

► HINT. Show what a good sport you are by making a set of vests to designate the opposing teams at a sports event. Make each team a different color and customize them with the team name or individual numbers.

Nylon Kite with Appliquéd UFO Design

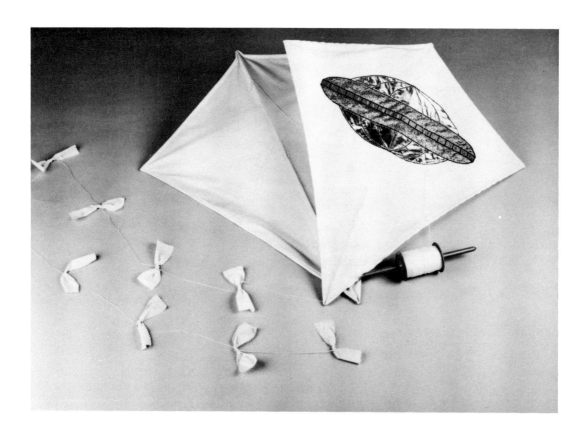

MATERIALS:

1 yard 44"-wide sky blue nylon fabric
Small scraps black, gray, and silver fabric for the appliqué
¼" wooden dowel
   One 36" piece
   One 32" piece
⅛" wooden dowel
   Three 36" pieces
¼ yard fabric fuser
Blue and black thread
Kite string

DIRECTIONS:

Pattern. A 20″ × 44″ piece of paper is needed to make a pattern. Tape the tops of 2 sections of newspaper together to make a large sheet. Use a colored felt tip pen to draw the pattern on the newspaper so it can be seen easily.

Draw a 39½″ line down the edge of the paper. This line will become the mast or vertical center of the kite. At a point 9″ from one end of the mast line, draw a 17½″ perpendicular line or spar line across the paper. Draw a line that connects the end of the spar line to one end of the mast line. Repeat this on the other side of the spar line.

Cutting. Fold the fabric in half along the cross grain, matching the selvage edges. Place the pattern on the fabric so the mast line is on the fold of the fabric. Pin the pattern to the doubled fabric and cut the kite out. Remove the pattern and open the kite out flat. Use pinking shears to cut six 2″ × 8″ pieces to use as bows for the kite's tail.

Appliqué. The UFO appliqué is stitched in the center of the kite on the right side of the fabric. One quarter of the design is given. Fold a 14″ × 14″ piece of tracing paper into fourths. Transfer the design to each quarter, matching the centers as indicated.

Trace the appliqué pieces of the design to a separate piece of paper. Cut each piece out from the appropriate color of scrap fabric. Back each piece with fabric fuser and position it in place on the center of the kite. Butt the fabric raw edges directly up against each other. The dotted lines on the illustration indicate pieces that are placed on top of other pieces. Fuse the appliqué pieces in place and satin stitch them in black thread as described under Machine Appliquéd Letters in Chapter 1.

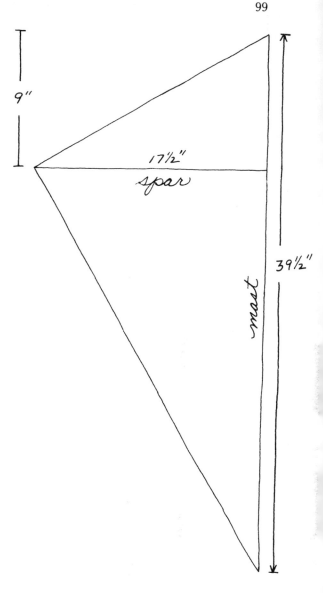

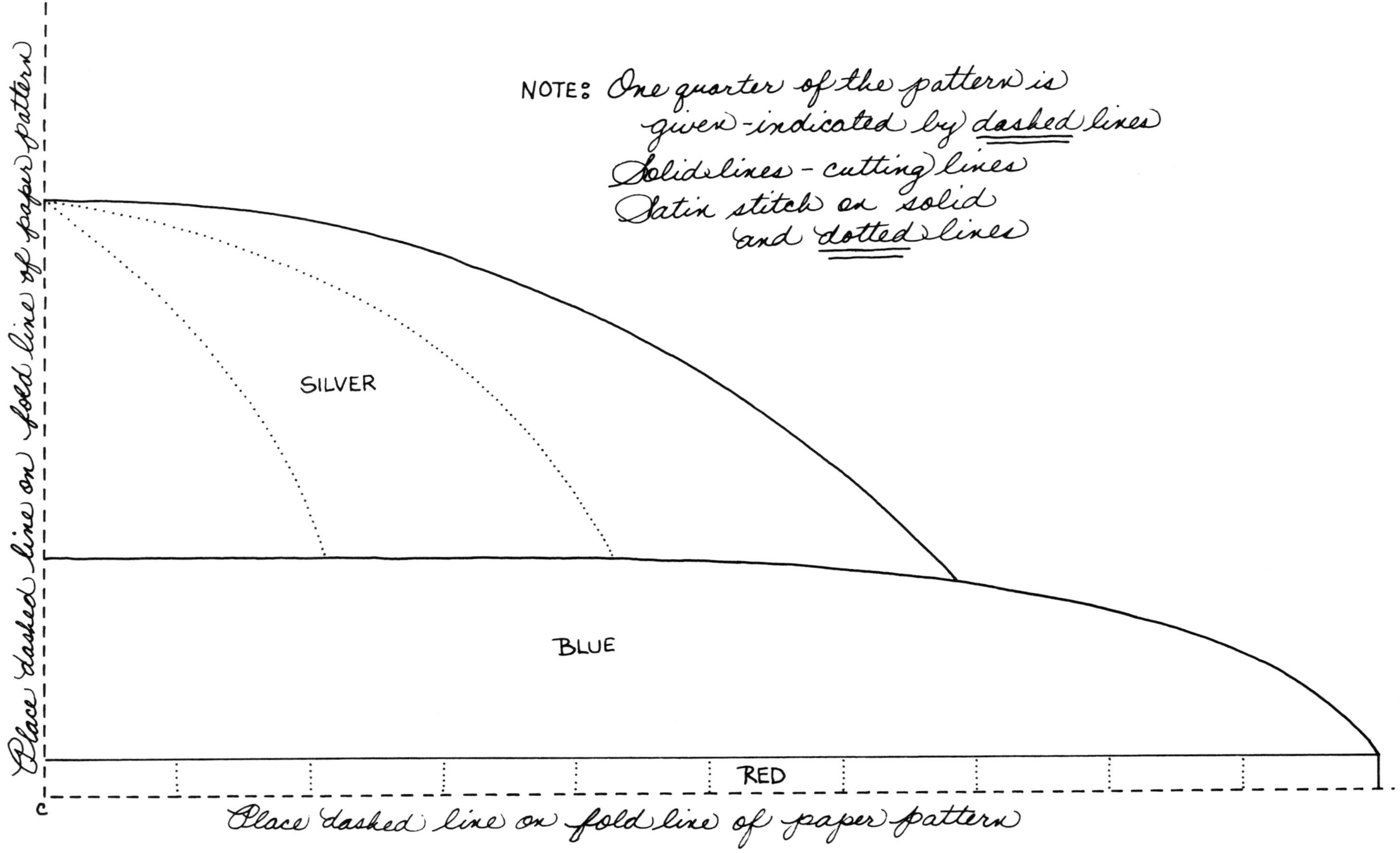

Place dashed line on fold line of paper pattern

c

SILVER

BLUE

RED

NOTE: One quarter of the pattern is
given - indicated by dashed line
Solid lines - cutting lines
Satin stitch on solid
and dotted lines

Place dashed line on fold line of paper pattern

Assembly. The edges of the kite are hemmed to finish the edge as well as provide pockets for the ends of the mast and spar sticks. Each corner pocket is formed by folding different amounts of fabric to the wrong side. For the top mast pocket of the kite, press ½" to the wrong side and then press ½" over again. Baste the folded edge of the pocket to the kite. The left and right spar pockets are first folded ½" and then 1". The lower mast pocket is folded 1" and then 1½". Baste all pockets in place as before.

Press under ½" on all the straight edges of the kite. Turn ½" under again and pin the hem to the kite along the folded edge. Machine edgestitch the straight folded edges of the hems in blue thread. Secure the thread ends neatly. Leave the diagonal ends of the hems open to insert the framing sticks.

The hems of the kite are framed out by the ⅛" dowel sticks. Slide one stick into each hem and cut it to fit snugly, about ⅛" shorter than the hem. Remove the basting from the corner pockets. Insert the mast and spar sticks into the corresponding corner pockets so they form a cross at the center. Trim the sticks if necessary so they stretch the kite fabric out tightly. Hand-stitch the ends of the hems closed to the corners, so they hold all of the sticks securely. Use a piece of kite string to lash the sticks together where they cross. Wrap the string around the sticks in an X and tie the ends well.

Hand-tack the kite to the mast stick every 8", using doubled blue thread. Insert the needle from the wrong side next to the stick, leaving an 8" end. Take a ¼" stitch on the right side of the kite. Return the needle to the wrong side and repeat. Knot the ends of the thread together tightly around the mast stick.

Tail. Cut a 6-foot length of kite string. Knot the 6 tail bow pieces tightly on the

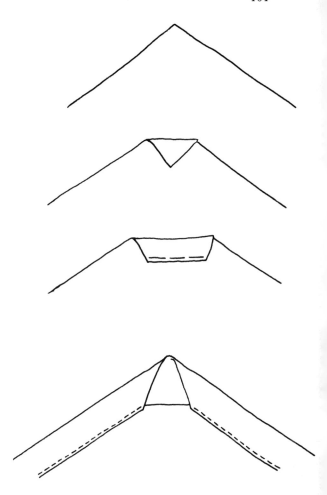

string, spacing them evenly. Make a knot in the kite string just below each bow so that it does not slip off. It is necessary to test fly the kite and adjust the tail length according to the kite's performance. The tail is intended to stabilize the flight of the kite and the length will vary according to fabric, weight, and wind.

Insert one end of the tail string into a large-eyed needle. On the wrong side of the kite, insert it through the kite next to the mast stick at a point 1 " above the bottom point of the kite. Take a ¼ " stitch on the right side, inserting the needle back on the other side of the stick. Tie the string around the stick.

Kite Line. Cut a 44 " length of kite string. Thread it into a large-eyed needle. On the right side of the kite, insert it to the wrong side at a point 10 " up from the bottom point of the kite. Pass it around the mast stick and return to the right side of the kite. Tie the end of the string tightly against the kite. Repeat this at a point 5 " down from the top point of the kite. Fold the string at a point 15 " from the upper connection to the kite. Make an overhand knot with the doubled thread 3 " from the fold, forming the bridle. Attach the end of the reel of kite string to this loop securely.

► **HINT.**   Besides being lots of fun, kites make great wall decorations for a boy's room when they're not being used. Hang one in a corner high up against the ceiling. Appliqué your favorite young high flyer's name on the kite for a really special surprise.

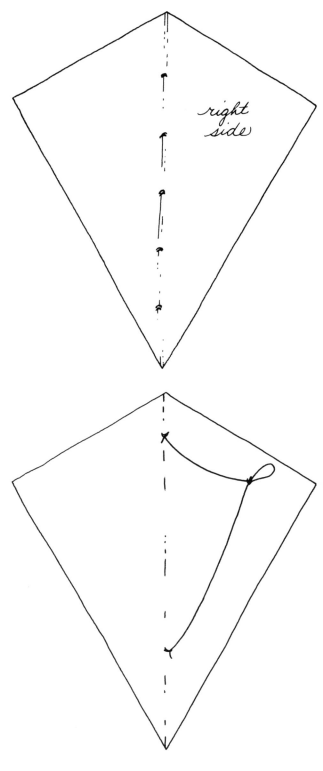

5.

Make It to Wear

Denim Work Apron with Hardware Details

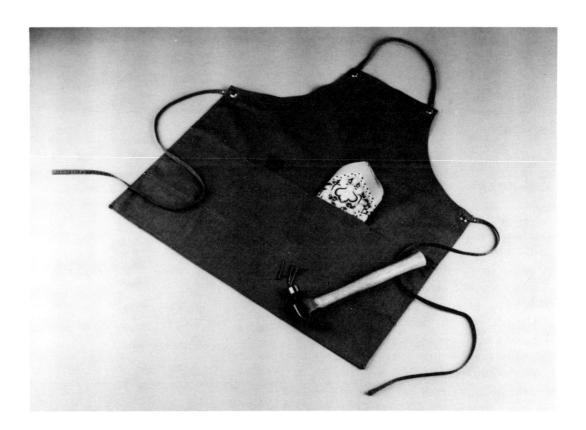

MATERIALS:

1½ yards denim fabric
20 brass rivets and setting tool
5 large grommets and setting tool
Bright orange thread

DIRECTIONS:

Cutting. From the denim, cut one 31"
× 31" apron piece and one 14" × 31"
pocket piece. Both upper corners of the
apron are curved to form a bib section.
Draw a 19" circle on a piece of paper and
cut it out. Fold the circle into quarters and
mark the fold lines in pencil. Position the
circle on one upper corner of the apron
piece so one quarter of the circle is placed
on top of the fabric. The fold lines of the
circle should be even with the raw edges
of the fabric. Pin it in place and draw the
curve on the fabric. Repeat this on the other
upper corner of the apron. Cut the fabric
on the curved lines.

Cut one 8" × 10½" top pocket piece.
Cut one 1½" × 24" neck loop and two
1½" × 41" waist ties.

Divided Pocket. Overcast one 31" edge
of the pocket piece. Along the overcast
edge, press ½" of fabric to the wrong side.
Working from the right side, make a row
of topstitching ⅛" from the folded edge.
Stitch a second row spaced ¼" from the
first row.

Fold the pocket in half and then into
quarters, creasing each fold line with your
iron. Open the pocket out and position it
on the apron with the right sides facing up.
Baste the side and bottom raw edges of the
pocket and the apron together.

The pocket is divided into 4 sections.
Beginning at the bottom edge, stitch along
one crease line up to the top of the pocket.
Pivot and stitch back to the hem, spacing
the second line of stitching ¼" away from
the first. Repeat on the remaining two
crease lines.

The bottom of the divided pocket is
formed by stitching. Draw a chalk line 6"
above and parallel to the hem edge of the
apron. Stitch through both thicknesses on
top of the chalk line and make a second row
¼" away as before.

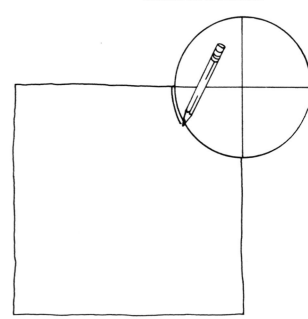

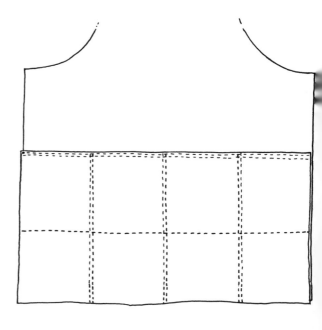

Top Pocket. The bottom of the pocket is cut to form a chevron shape. Make a mark on each 10½" edge that is 1" above the bottom of the pocket. Draw a line connecting each mark to the center of the pocket bottom. Cut on the lines.

Overcast the top 8" edge of the pocket. Fold 2½" toward the right side of the pocket, forming a facing. Stitch both sides of the facing to the pocket as described under the Terry Bathwrap in Chapter 2. Trim the facing seam allowances and turn the facing right side out. Press flat and topstitch the facing as you did the lower pocket. Repeat the 2 rows of topstitching 2" down from the top of the pocket. Press under ½" on all remaining raw edges.

Center the pocket on the bib section of the apron so it is 2" down from and parallel to the top of the apron. Topstitch the side and pointed bottom to the apron, using a double row of stitching as before.

Ties. Make the neck loop by folding the 1½" × 24" piece in half lengthwise. Press ½" to the wrong side on both short ends of the neck tie. With the right sides together, match the long raw edges, making sure the pressed-under edges are even, and machine stitch. Use a small safety pin to turn the loop right side out. Press it flat and edgestitch along both edges. Make 2 waist ties just as you did the neck loop.

Assembly. Overcast all the raw edges on the apron. Press them to the wrong side and topstitch as you did before. Insert grommets in the upper corners of the bib section and the upper side corners of the apron. Follow the manufacturer's instructions carefully. Make a test insertion on scrap fabric. If extra thickness is needed, cut a scrap piece of fabric to back the spots where the grommets are being inserted. Insert one end of each waist tie into the grommet from the right side on the upper side corners. Fold 2" of the tie to the wrong side

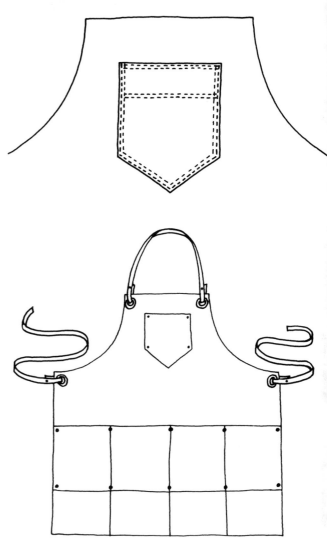

and secure the tie by inserting a rivet through both layers. Insert one end of the neck loop into each grommet at the bib corners. Pin the ends to the wrong side of the loop, making sure it is not twisted. Secure the neck loop ends as you did the waist ties.

Also insert a rivet on all pocket corners, at the top and bottom. Follow the manufacturer's instructions carefully for inserting rivets.

► **HINT.** For a great souvenir of your next family picnic or reunion, make this up for the barbecue chef. Use natural off-white canvas fabric and have everyone autograph it with permanent felt tip markers.

Gourmet Apron to Sew and Embroider

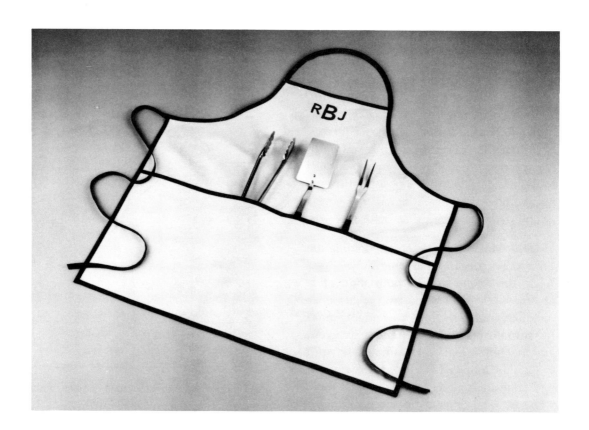

MATERIALS:

1½ yards natural color lightweight canvas
7 yards 1″-wide rust bias tape
1 skein 6-strand rust embroidery floss
Letter monogram transfer or pattern
Thread to match the fabric
Thread to match the bias tape

DIRECTIONS:

Cutting. From the canvas, cut one 31″ × 31″ apron and one 14″ × 31″ pocket piece. Shape the bib section of the apron as described under the Denim Work Apron.

Divided Pocket. Bind the top 31″ edge of the pocket piece with the rust bias tape, as described under Racket Covers in Chapter 4. Divide the pocket into quarters and apply it to the apron as described under the Denim Work Apron.

Assembly. Bind the top edge of the bib section with bias tape. Finish the hem edge of the apron by binding all thicknesses of the fabric with bias tape. Next bind the side edges of the apron, finishing the corners at the hem edge by turning under ½″ of bias tape.

The curved edges of the apron are bound with one piece of bias tape that forms the neck loop and the waist ties at the same time. Beginning at one side edge, leave a 39″ length of bias as a waist tie and then bind the curved edge. At the top, leave 18″ of bias tape free for the neck loop. Test the length of the neck loop and adjust if necessary. Make sure that the bias tape is not twisted. Bind the remaining curved edge as before, leaving a 39″ tie end at the waistline corner.

Press the bias tape in half for the neck loop and waist ties. Press under ½″ of bias tape at each end of the waist ties. To finish the neck loop and waist ties, press the bias tape in half, matching the prefolded edges. Edgestitch both edges of the bias tape neck loop and waist ties.

Monogram. Follow the instructions in Chapter 1 to satin stitch a monogram to the center of the apron bib section. Place the top of the monogram 1″ below the binding at the top of the bib.

►**Hint.** This design makes a good all-purpose plastic apron. Use clear plastic or a nice color of vinyl and omit the monogram.

Ragg Knitted Hat

MATERIALS:

1 skein 4-ply yarn
No. 8 knitting needles

DIRECTIONS:

This knitted hat is worked from the top of the hat toward the ribbed cuff.

Gauge—Stockinette stitch: 4 sts = 1″
    6 rows = 1″

Cast on 76 stitches.

Pattern Stitch.

Row 1: Knit across the row.
Row 2: Purl across the row.
Repeat rows 1 and 2 for 6″.

Ribbing.

All rows: K 2, P 2.

Repeat the ribbing row for 6″. Bind off loosely. Lightly steam the completed piece so that it is flat.

Seam the short ends of the hat together to form a tube. With the right sides together, match the 2 short ends. Starting at the top edge, stitch the edges together, stopping at the beginning of the ribbing. Do *not* end the yarn. Turn the hat right side out and continue sewing the seam with the wrong sides placed together. When the hat is worn the ribbing is turned up and the seam will be concealed on the wrong side.

Finishing. Cut a 12″ length of yarn. Work a running stitch around the top edge of the hat, picking up every third stitch. Pull on the yarn to close the opening. Secure the yarn end to prevent the closing from opening.

▶ HINT. Make this hat up in a dark, solid color and add small, cross-stitch initials in a contrasting color. Position them 1½″ above the ribbing at the center front of the hat.

PROJECT
Simple Scarf for Beginners to Knit

MATERIALS:

3 skeins 4-ply yard
No. 8 knitting needles
Size F crochet hook

DIRECTIONS:

This scarf is knitted with the garter stitch. Cast on 48 stitches.

Gauge—Garter stitch: 4 sts = 1"
6 rows = 1"

Row 1: Knit across the row

Continue knitting each row until the scarf is the desired length. A sporty scarf is usually 60" long. A dress scarf is generally 40" long.

When the desired length is reached, bind off.

Fringe can be added as a finishing touch if desired. To make the fringe, wind yarn lengthwise around a paperback book until a ½"-thick bundle is formed. Cut the yarn at one end of the book. Each fringe tassel consists of 3 strands of yarn. Repeat winding and cutting yarn until you have enough strands for the fringe. Divide the lengths of yarn into groups of 3. Fold each group in half and, using a crochet hook, draw the folded end through one stitch at the edge of the scarf. Draw the yarn ends through the loop and pull to tighten it. Insert one yarn group in the first and last stitches. The remaining yarn groups are inserted at ¼" intervals. Repeat fringing on the opposite end of the scarf. After the fringe is applied, trim all the ends so that they are even.

► HINT. Four 60" scarves, seamed together, make a great afghan. Make 2 in one color and 2 in another. Stitch them together on the 60" side to form alternating stripes. Add matching fringe to the top and bottom edges.

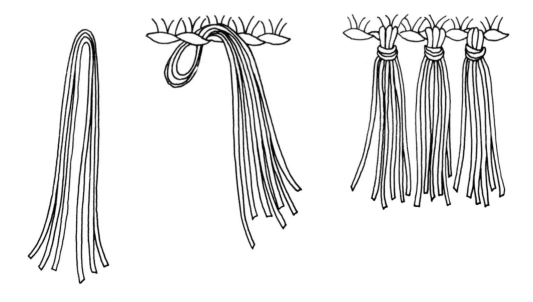

Kimono-style Terry Bathrobe for Men and Boys

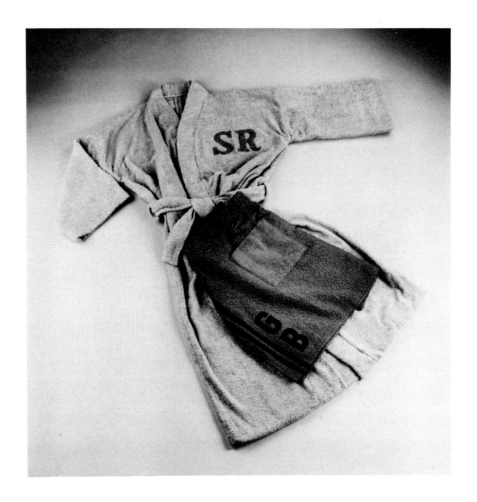

MATERIALS:

3¾ yards (3 yards) blue terry cloth
Thread to match fabric

Racket Covers *page 86*

Thermos Carrier *page 52*

Pillows Made from Dyed Handkerchieves *page 149*

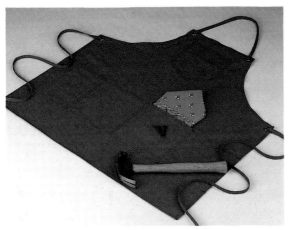

Denim Work Apron with Hardware Details
page 103

Comforter from Old Shirts   *page 152*

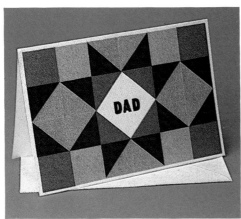

Father's Day Card of Sandpaper Patchwork
page 40

**Happy Birthday Card with
Paper Cutwork**   *page 43*

Journals to Cover and Personalize
page 29

Ragg Knitted Hat   *page 108*

Laundry Bag *page 177*

Knit Scarf for Beginners *page 110*

Silky Aviator's Scarf *page 34*

Portable Spectator's Cushion *page 67*

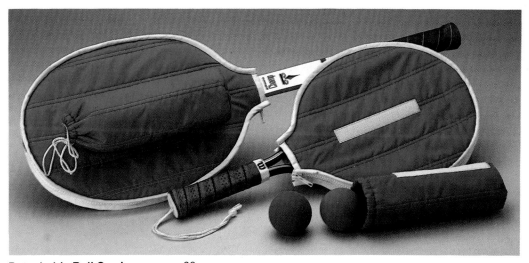

Detachable Ball Carriers *page 89*

Crocheted Golf Club Covers with Cross-stitch
page 92

Hand-embroidered Monogramming for Purchased Ties *page 19*

Easy Pillows from Felt Pennants
page 142

Knitted Aran Pattern Scarf *page 122*

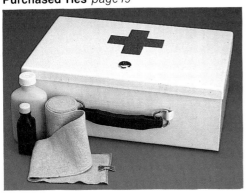

First Aid Kit *page 164*

Chessboard Made with Ceramic Tiles *page 71;*
Chess Set to Assemble with Corks *page 73*

Traveling Backgammon Board *page 80*

Crocheted Stadium Blanket
page 54

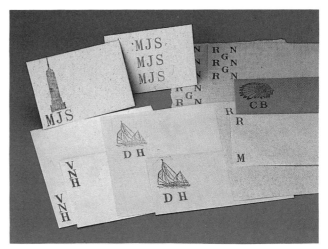

Stationery with Stamped Designs   *page 24*

Light-reflective Vest   *page 95*

Paper Portfolio   *page 26*

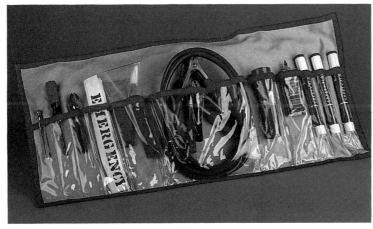

Roll-up Tool Kit for Car   *page 47*

Two-color Scarf   *page 38*

Personalized Accessories *page 15*

Picture Frames from Newspaper Strips *page 156*

Eyeglass Cases *pag*

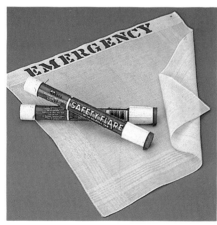

Emergency Stenciled Handkerchief *page 50*

Gift Wrap, Ribbon, to Make with Rubber Stamps *page 21*

Knitted Tie *page 115*

Stenciled Beach Chair *page 160*

Two-tone Wool Scarf *page 36*

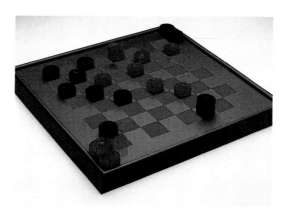

Checkerboard *page 76*

Office Organizer *page 185*

Tobacco-jar Pipe Caddy *page 131*

Items Papered with Maps *page 138*

Initialed Bathwrap *page 31*
Initialed Bathrobe *page 112*

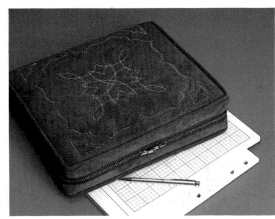

Zippered Binder with Western-style Stitching
page 57

Crocheted Alma Mater Pillow
page 140

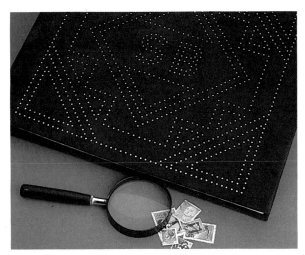

Album   *page 144*

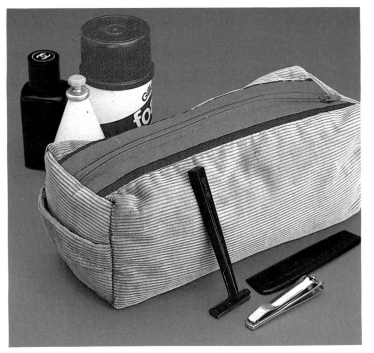

Zippered Shaving Kit   *page 180*

Collage I Love You Card   *pag*

DIRECTIONS:

NOTE. Changes for boys size are given in parentheses. Boys size will fit a boy approximately 4½′ to 5′ tall.

Cutting. Cut the following pieces from the terry cloth:

Four 15″ × 54″ (11″ × 41″) fronts and backs

Two 18″ × 22″ (15″ × 18″) sleeves

Two 6″ × 61″ (4″ × 45″) front/neck-bands

Two 6″ × 41″ (4″ × 28″) tie belt

Two 2″ × 6½″ (2″ × 4½″) belt loops

(To make the Terry Bathwrap see page 31.)

Neckline Shaping. The upper corners of the 2 front pieces are cut at an angle to form a wrap-style neckline. On the right side of the fabric, measure 4″ (3″) along one 15″ (11″) edge of one front piece. Working from the same corner, mark a point 9″ (8″) down along the 54″ (41″) side. Draw a chalk line connecting the 2 marks and cut on the line. Slightly round the corner at the 9″ (8″) mark by drawing around the edge of a saucer and cutting on the line. Repeat this on the right side of the other front piece, making sure that you have both a left and a right front piece.

Assembly. With right sides together, match the 2 back pieces along one long edge. Pin and stitch this edge, forming the center back seam. Press the seam open and overcast the raw edges.

Match the front pieces to the joined back at the shoulder seams. Place right sides together with the shaped neckline edges directed toward the center. Pin each shoulder seam, stopping at a point ½″ from the neckline edge. Stitch, press the seams open, and overcast the raw edges.

Sleeves. Mark the center of one 22″ (18″) side on each sleeve. With right sides together, match the center of each sleeve piece to one shoulder seam of the robe. Pin

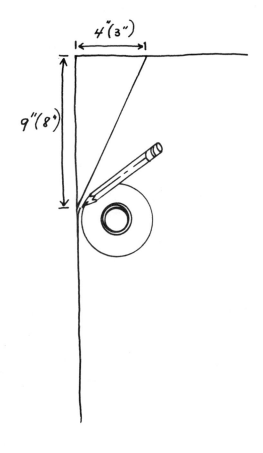

and stitch the sleeves to the robe. Trim the sleeve seams to ¼" and overcast them together. Press the seam allowances toward the sleeve.

Belt Loops. With right sides together, fold each belt loop in half lengthwise, matching the long raw edges. Stitch the seam and trim the seam allowance to ¼". Use a safety pin to turn each loop right side out. Press the loops flat. Fold the loop in half, matching the raw edges. Position them on the robe back at the side seam 8" (5½") down from the sleeve seam. Match the raw edges of the loop to the raw edge of the robe.

Make sure that the loop is not twisted. Baste it in place. Repeat on the other side seam.

Neckband. With right sides together, seam the two 6" (4") ends of the neckband pieces together. Press the seam open. Fold the band in half lengthwise, placing the wrong sides together. Match the raw edges and baste them together. Pin the raw edges of the band to the front and neckline edges of the robe. Match the neckband seam to the center back of the robe. Machine-stitch, trim the seam allowances to ¼", and overcast. Press the seam allowances toward the robe.

Finishing. With right sides together, match the underarm and side seams of the front to the back. Pin and stitch the seams, securing the belt loops at the same time. Press the seams open and overcast the raw edges. Overcast the raw edges at the sleeve and hemline. Press ½" toward the wrong side. Pin and make 2 rows of topstitching to hold the hems in place. Place the first row ⅛" in from the edge and the second ¼" in from the first row.

Belt. With right sides together, seam the 2 belt sections together, matching them at one short end. Press the seam open. With right sides together, fold the belt in half lengthwise. Match the raw edges and machine-stitch the ends and length of the belt, leaving a 6" opening at the center. Trim the seam allowances to ¼", turn the belt right side out, and press it flat, tucking in the seam allowances at the opening. Hand slip-stitch the opening closed. Make 2 rows of topstitching around the entire belt as you did on the hems.

►**Hint.** Make a shorter version of the bathrobe in luxurious quilted fabric to be worn as a smoking jacket. Simply cut the man's 4 front and back pieces 15" × 37" and complete the jacket in the same way as the robe.

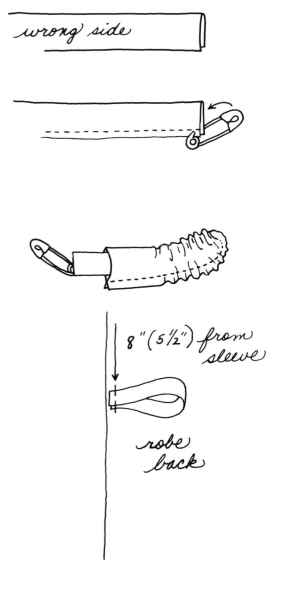

wrong side

8" (5½") from sleeve

robe back

PROJECT
Knitted Tie with Diagonal Twill Design

MATERIALS:

1 skein fingering-weight burgundy cotton
No. 2 knitting needles
Size C crochet hook
3" × 54" strip of voile interfacing

DIRECTIONS:

The tie is knitted in one piece. The finished width is 2½" at the widest point and 52" long.

Before starting, make a swatch to test the gauge. The swatch is also useful in helping you become acquainted with the stitch pattern. Also, it might be a good idea to practice decreasing without losing your place in the pattern.

Gauge—Pattern stitch: 7 sts = 1"
     10 rows = 1"

Pattern.

Row 1: * K 4, P 1. Repeat from * across row.

Row 2: * P 1, K 1, P 3. Repeat from * across row.

Row 3: * K 2, P 1, K 2. Repeat from * across row.

Row 4: * P 3, K 1, P 1. Repeat from * across row.

Row 5: * P 1, K 4. Repeat from * across row.

Row 6: * K 1, P 4. Repeat from * across row.

Row 7: * K 3, P 1, K 1. Repeat from * across row.

Row 8: * P 2, K 1, P 2. Repeat from * across row.

Row 9: * K 1, P 1, K 3. Repeat from * across row.

Row 10:* P 4, K 1. Repeat from * across row.

Cast on 35 stitches.

Following the pattern, work even for 30 rows. Beginning with the next row, decrease 1 stitch each side every 20 rows 7 times. There are 19 stitches remaining. Work the remaining 19 stitches in pattern until the tie measures 52". Bind off.

Finishing. Block the tie so that it measures 52" in length. Trim the interfacing to fit in the center of the tie and hand-tack it in place on the wrong side.

With wrong sides together, seam the long edges of the tie using a whip stitch. Press the tie so that the seam is in the middle of the back side of the tie.

The bottom of the tie is closed by crocheting the edges together with a single crochet.

►**Hint.**   For a sporty tweed effect using this pattern select a flecked or heather-colored yarn. To make the design appear more elegant, pick out a yarn with a slight sheen or luster.

Tie to Crochet with Easy Stitches

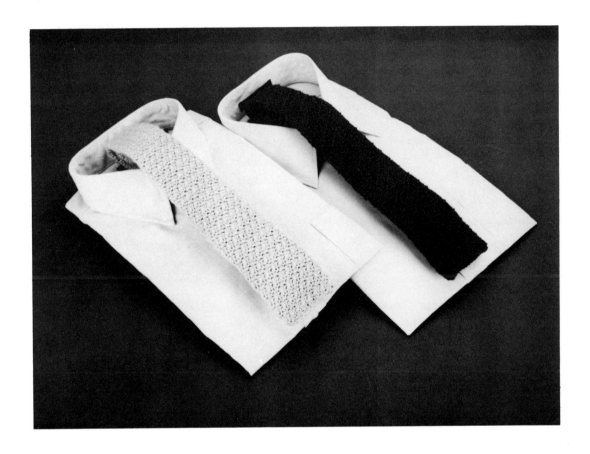

MATERIALS:

1 skein fingering-weight gold cotton yarn
Size C crochet hook
3″ × 54″ strip of voile interfacing

DIRECTIONS:

The tie is crocheted in one piece. The finished dimensions are the same as the knitted tie.

Before starting, make a swatch to test the gauge. The swatch is useful in helping you become acquainted with the pattern and you can also use the swatch to practice decreasing.

Gauge: 6 sts = 1″   6 rows = 1″

Pattern.

Row 1: Sk 2 ch, 1 sc in next ch, * 1 dc, 1 sc *. Repeat from * to * across the row to last ch, 1 dc. Ch 2, turn.

Row 2: Sk 1 st dc, * 1 dc in sc of previous row, 1 sc in dc of previous row *. Repeat from * to * across the row to the ch 2 of the previous row, 1 dc in ch 2 of previous row. Ch 2, turn.

Repeat from row 2 for pattern.

Chain 32.

Following the pattern, work even for 18 rows. Beginning with the next row, decrease 1 stitch each side every 9 rows, 8 times. There are 16 remaining stitches.

Work the remaining 16 stitches in the pattern until the tie measures 52″.

Fasten off.

Finishing. For finishing, see the Knitted Tie directions.

► Hint. Use 3 or 4 colors of yarn to make a classy striped variation of this tie. Work 2 rows in each color and then repeat the colors in the same sequence over and over again, following the instructions.

Classic Hat with Knitted Aran Pattern

MATERIALS:

One 3½-ounce skein 4-ply worsted yarn
No. 8 knitting needles
1 cable needle

DIRECTIONS:

Gauge—Stockinette stitch: 4 sts = 1″
  6 rows = 1″

Before beginning, check your gauge by knitting a 4″ × 4″ square of stockinette stitch. Adjust your needle size to obtain correct gauge.

Aran knitting consists of several different stitches to form a very patterned and textured surface. This Aran hat uses the coiled cable, popcorn, and diamond patterns.

The hat is worked from the top edge of the hat toward the ribbed cuff.

Abbreviations.

CN: Cable Needle

Cr2F: Slip next st onto cable needle and leave at *front* of work, K 1, then K 1 from cable needle.

C2F: Slip next st onto cable needle and leave at *front* of work. P 1, then K 1 from cable needle.

C2B: Slip next st onto cable needle and leave at *back* of work, K 1, then P 1 from cable needle.

Cast on 76 sts.

Row 1: K 1, P 3, K 1, P 2, sl 4 sts onto CN and leave at *front* of work, K 4, then K 4 sts from CN, P 2, K 1, P 3, K 1, P 2 (K into front and back of next st 5 times, then sl the 2nd, 3rd, 4th, and 5th sts over the first—1 popcorn made), P 2, K 1, P 3, K 1, P 5, Cr2F, P 5, K 1, P 3, K 1, P 2, make one popcorn in the next st, P 2, K 1, P 3, K 1, P 2, sl 4 sts onto CN and leave at *front* of work, K 4, then K 4 sts from CN, P 2, K 1, P 3, K 1.

Row 2: P 1, K 3, P 1, K 2, P 8, K 2, P 1, K 3, P 1, K 5, P 1, K 3, P 1, K 5, P 2, K 5, P 1, K 3, P 1, K 5, P 1, K 3, P 1, K 2, P 8, K 2, P 1, K 3, P 1.

Row 3: K 1, P 3, K 1, P 2, K 8, P 2, K 1, P 3, K 1, P 5, K 1, P 3, K 1, P 4, C2B, C2F, P 4, K 1, P 3, K 1, P 5, K 1, P 3, K 1, P 2, K 8, P 2, K 1, P 3, K 1.

Row 4: P 1, K 3, P 1, K 2, P 8, K 2, P 1, K 3, P 1, K 5, P 1, K 3, P 1, K 4, P 1, K 2, P 1, K 4, P 1, K 3, P 1, K 5, P 1, K 3, P 1, K 2, P 8, K 2, P 1, K 3, P 1.

Row 5: K 1, P 3, K 1, P 2, K 8, P 2, K 1, P 3, K 1, P 5, K 1, P 3, K 1, P 3, C2B, P 2, C2F, P 3, K 1, P 3, K 1, P 5, K 1, P 3, K 1, P 2, K 8, P 2, K 1, P 3, K 1.

Row 6: P 1, K 3, P 1, K 2, P 8, K 2, P 1, K 3, P 1, K 5, P 1, K 3, P 1, K 3, P 1, K 4, P 1, K 3, P 1, K 3, P 1, K 5, P 1, K 3, P 1, K 2, P 8, K 2, P 1, K 3, P 1.

Row 7: K 1, P 3, K 1, P 2, K 8, P 2, K 1, P 3, K 1, P 5, K 1, P 3, K 1, P 2, C2B, P 4, C2F, P 2, K 1, P 3, K 1, P 5, K 1, P 3, K 1, P 2, K 8, P 2, K 1, P 3, K 1.

Row 8: P 1, K 3, P 1, K 2, P 8, K 2, P 1, K 3, P 1, K 5, P 1, K 3, P 1, K 2, P 1, K 6, P 1, K 2, P 1, K 3, P 1, K 5, P 1, K 3, P 1, K 2, P 8, K 2, P 1, K 3, P 1.

Row 9: K 1, P 3, K 1, P 2, sl 4 sts onto CN and leave at *front* of work, K 4, then K 4 sts from CN, P 2, K 1, P 3, K 1, P 2, make 1 popcorn in next st, P 2, K 1, P 3, K 1, P 2, C2F, P 4, C2B, P 2, K 1, P 3, K 1, P 2, make 1 popcorn in next st, P 2, K 1, P 3, K 1, P 2, sl 4 sts onto CN and leave at *front* of work, K 4, then K 4 sts from CN, P 2, K 1, P 3, K 1.

Row 10: Repeat row 6.

Row 11: K 1, P 3, K 1, P 2, K 8, P 2,
K 1, P 3, K 1, P 5, K 1, P 3, K 1,
P 3, C2F, P 2, C2B, P 3, K 1, P 3,
K 1, P 5, K 1, P 3, K 1, P 2, K 8,
P 2, K 1, P 3, K 1.

Row 12: Repeat row 4.

Row 13: K 1, P 3, K 1, P 2, K 8, P 2,
K 1, P 3, K 1, P 5, K 1, P 3, K 1,
P 4, C2F, C2B, P 4, K 1, P 3, K 1,
P 5, K 1, P 3, K 1, P 2, K 8, P 2,
K 1, P 3, K 1.

Row 14: Repeat row 2.

Row 15: Repeat row 1.

Row 16: Repeat row 2.

Work the hat for a length of 6 ". Repeat
rows 1 to 16 as needed, ending on a number 8 row.

Change to ribbing to finish the hat.
Work the ribbing for 6 ". Follow the ribbing and finishing directions given under
the Ragg Knitted Hat.

► **Hint.** Knit this hat in a bright color
for your favorite skier. Make a large pom-
pom as described under the Golf Club
Cover in Chapter 4 and attach it to the
gathered top of the hat.

Aran Pattern Scarf to Knit

MATERIALS:

Three 3½-ounce skeins 4-ply gray worsted yarn
No. 8 knitting needles
1 cable needle
Size F crochet hook

DIRECTIONS:

The Aran pattern for the scarf is the same
as the Classic Hat pattern.

Gauge—Stockinette stitch: 4 sts = 1"
6 rows = 1"

Follow the directions for the hat, repeat-
ing rows 1 to 16 until you have reached
your desired length. End with a number 16
row. The scarf measures 44" long and has
17 pattern repeats. Bind off at the desired
length. Block the scarf to approximately 15"
× 44".

If desired, add fringe to each end of the
scarf, following directions under the Simple Scarf.

► HINT. This knitted pattern can be
used to make a handsome pillow. Work the
pattern stitch until your piece measures
30". Bind off and seam the 15" ends
together, forming a loop. Fold the piece flat
at the seam and crochet the side edges
together. Leave a small opening on one side
and stuff the pillow before closing it up.
Add fringe at the 2 sides if desired.

Bow Tie to Make from Velvet Ribbon

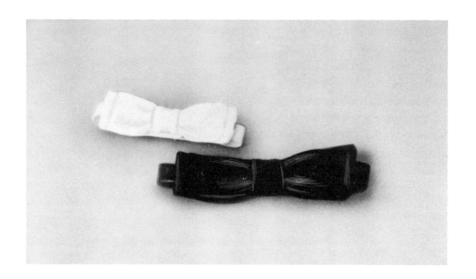

MATERIALS: (Changes for boys are given in parentheses)

¾ yard 2 "-wide black (white) velvet ribbon
¾ yard ¼ "-wide black (white) satin ribbon
½ yard ¾ "-wide elastic
One large snap
Thread to match the velvet ribbon

DIRECTIONS:

Bow. The ribbon tie is made separately and then tacked to a piece of elastic that fits around the neck. Appliqué the ¼"-wide satin ribbon to the center of the velvet ribbon. Cut a 20" (16") length of ribbon. Fold the ribbon in half crosswise so that the wrong sides are together. Tack the ribbon together at a point that is 4" (3½") from the cut ends. Flatten out the loop that is formed and tack it down at the center, forming the bow. The ribbon ends should be in a pressed-open position.

Cut a 3" length of ribbon for the knot of the bow. Press under ½" on each 3" side edge. Wrap the ribbon vertically around the center of the bow. Pull it tightly, allowing the bow to gather naturally. Turn under ½" on one raw end of the ribbon and lap it over the remaining raw edge of the ribbon. Tack securely.

Finishing. Stitch the bow to the center of the elastic. Trim the elastic to fit the neck size, allowing extra for a 1" overlap. Sew the snap on the overlap. Fold the raw edge of the ends of the ribbon to the wrong side so that only about ¼" extends beyond the bow. Trim off any excess ribbon and hand-tack the raw edges invisibly.

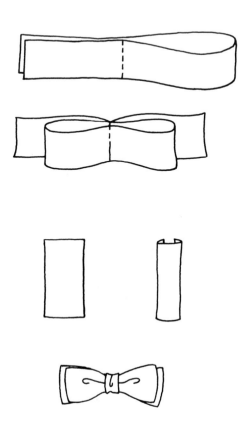

► **Hint.** Make up the tie and cummerbund set for the male members of a wedding party. Select colors to coordinate with the bride and bridesmaid's colors.

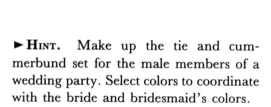

Suspenders for Fun and Fancy Occasions

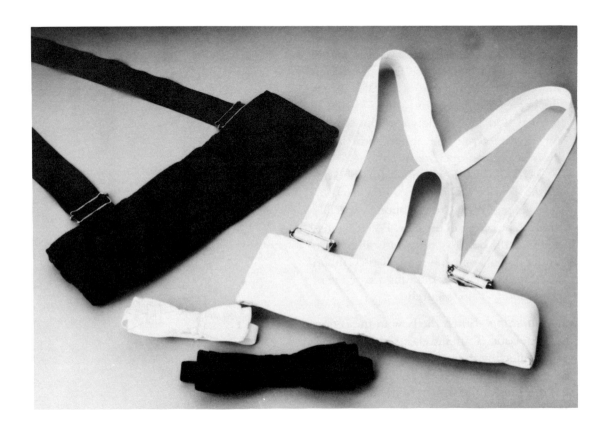

MATERIALS: (Changes for boys are given in parentheses)

3 yards (2¼ yards) 2″ (1½″)-wide black (white) satin ribbon
3 yards (2¼ yards) ⅜″-wide black (white) velvet ribbon
2 suspender buckles
2 suspender buttons
2 black (white) plastic buttons
Matching thread
(To make the bow ties see page 124)

DIRECTIONS:

Suspender Straps. The suspender strap is composed of 3 lengths of ribbon stitched together. Center the narrow velvet ribbon on top of the wide satin ribbon. The ⅜″-wide velvet ribbon is appliquéd to the center of the 2″-wide satin ribbon. Baste and edgestitch the narrow ribbon in position.

Cut the strap in half crosswise to make 2 pieces. Press under ¼″ of 1 raw edge of each strap. Insert a suspender buckle onto this end. Fold approximately ¾″ to 1″ of the strap to the wrong side encasing the suspender buckle. Machine-stitch the pressed-under edge in place.

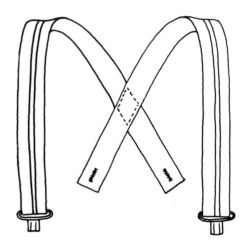

Finishing. Try on the suspenders with the cummerbund. Mark the positions for the suspender buttons on the cummerbund. The buttons will be sewn on the wrong side of the cummerbund approximately 10″ (7″) apart and 1¼″ (¾″) down from the top edge. Sew the suspender buttons in place.

The suspenders are crossed at the center back. Secure this point with pins and then machine-stitch. Adjust the length of the suspenders. Hem the ends of the suspenders by turning under ¼″ two times and stitching across the inner folded edge. Work buttonholes in each end to accommodate the plastic buttons. Sew the plastic buttons to the inside of the trouser waistband at the back to attach the suspender ends.

► **Hint.** Use striped elastic to make a pair of snappy suspenders. Wide elastic, striped in nice colors, is available for making stretch belts. Follow the instructions, omitting the velvet ribbons

Cummerbund Decorated with Velvet Ribbons

MATERIALS: (Changes for the boys are given in parentheses)

¼ yard black (white) satin fabric
¼ yard Thermolam fleece
¼ yard black (white) broadcloth
¾ yard (½ yard) black (white) 1″-wide elastic
1¼ yards (1 yard) each of 3 assorted widths of black (white) velvet ribbons
One swimsuit hook
Matching thread

DIRECTIONS:

Cutting. The cummerbund pattern is drawn from a rectangle. Cut a 6″ × 23″ (5″ × 20″) piece of paper. Fold the paper into quarters and mark the fold lines. Working in one corner, measure 6½″ in toward the center on the long edge and make a mark. Along the short edge, measure 1″ from the top and make a mark. Use a French curve to connect the marks. Fold the pattern into quarters and cut each corner to match the first one. Draw a line on the pattern that is at a 45-degree angle to the center front line. This is the ribbon placement guideline.

Use the pattern to cut one piece each of satin, fleece, and broadcloth. Transfer the ribbon guideline to the satin. With the right side up, layer the satin over the fleece and baste the layers together.

Assembly. Stitch the ribbon to the cummerbund front, starting at the placement guideline. Lay out the ribbons on the satin in the order of small, medium, and large widths. There is a ½″ space between each ribbon. Baste the ribbons in place, re-peating the sequence as often as necessary to cover the entire cummerbund. Edgestitch each ribbon in place through all thicknesses.

Back Closure. Cut two 11″ (9″) pieces of elastic for the back closure. Fold each piece in half. Insert the swimsuit hook onto one piece. Baste the raw ends of the elastic to the short ends of the cummerbund front. Spread the elastic so that each end is ½″ in from the corner. Try the cummerbund on and adjust the elastic if necessary for a proper fit.

Finishing. With the right sides together, pin the broadcloth to the cummerbund front. Stitch the outer raw edges together, securing the elastic ends. Leave a 6″ opening to turn. Trim the seam allowance to ¼″. Turn the cummerbund right side out and press the edges flat. Slip-stitch the opening closed.

► HINT. For a more conservative, for-mal look make up the tie and cummerbund in a subtle stripe or patterned fabric. Follow the instructions, omitting the velvet ribbons.

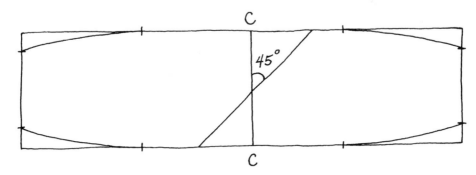

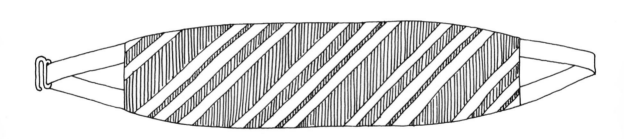

6.

Make It for the Den

PROJECT

Tobacco-Jar Pipe Caddy to Stitch

MATERIALS:

One 11″-tall 1½-quart canister-type jar with wooden lid
⅜ yard 44″-wide beige imitation suede
¼ yard ¼″-wide elastic
Heavy brown topstitching thread

DIRECTIONS:

Pattern. Measure the circumference of your jar and add 1 " to determine the width of the caddy pattern. Measure the height of the glass portion of the jar (with the lid on) and add 2 " to find the pattern height. Draw a rectangle to these dimensions. Cut the pattern out. Fold the pattern width into 8 equal sections and mark the fold lines to indicate pocket divisions.

Cut out a pipe pocket pattern that measures 7 " high × the caddy pattern width plus 8 " extra for pocket fullness. Fold the pattern into 8 equal sections and mark the fold lines to indicate pocket dividing lines.

Cutting. Use the patterns to cut one caddy piece and one pocket from the imitation suede. Transfer the pattern fold lines to each suede piece. Cut one 1½ " × 41 " tie drawstring.

Pocket. Turn a ¾ " pocket hem to the wrong side along one long edge of the pocket. Set your machine to a large stitch and, using the topstitching thread, make 2 rows of topstitching to secure the hem in place. Place them ⅛ " and then ¼ " in from the folded edge.

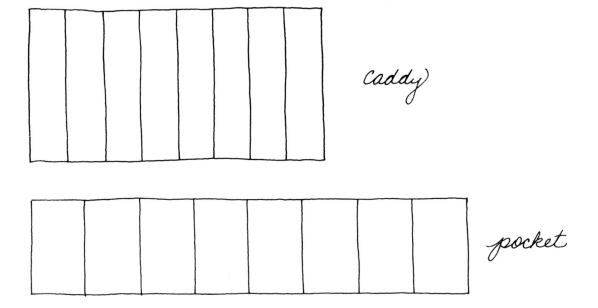

caddy

pocket

Transfer the stitching design to each of the 8 sections of the pocket piece. Position the stitch design so it intersects the second row of topstitching on the hemmed edge at each pocket dividing line. Topstitch on top of the stitching design lines. Begin at the raw edge of the pocket and stitch a diamond pattern, ending at the point where you began. Stitch until all pattern design lines are covered.

Assembly. The pocket piece is applied to the caddy piece and pleated in to form pipe pockets. Match the short sides of the pocket to the base piece at the side bottom edge. Machine-baste them together ¼"

from the raw edges. Match the marked pocket dividing lines on both pieces and baste them together. Center 2 rows of topstitching spaced ¼" apart over each pocket dividing line, as described under the Denim Work Apron in Chapter 5. Begin stitching at the bottom, pivot, forming a box of stitching at the pocket hem, and then return to the bottom edge.

Flatten each pocket to fit the caddy piece by forming a pleat at both lower corners of each pocket. The pleats from the adjoining pockets will meet and form a box pleat over the pocket dividing lines. Do not make pleats in the pockets at the ends of the caddy piece. Machine-baste the pleats in place ¼" from the bottom edge.

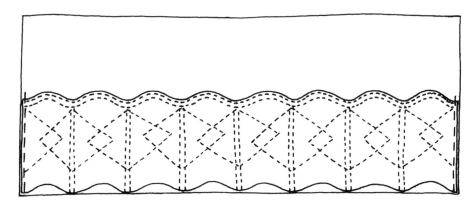

With right sides together match the 2 short ends of the combined caddy and pocket sections. Make sure the extra allowance for the 2 end pockets does not get caught in the seam. Stitch the seam and press it open. Topstitch the seam to resemble the other pocket dividing lines. Form the pleats for the pockets on each side of the seam as you did before.

To form the bottom casing, press ¾″ to the wrong side. Machine-stitch ½″ away from the folded edge, leaving a 1″ opening to insert the elastic. Insert the elastic with a small safety pin and adjust the length to fit your jar snugly. The casing will wrap around toward the bottom of the jar approximately ½″. Stitch the ends of the elastic together and close the casing.

To make the casing at the top, press 1″ to the wrong side. Edgestitch around the fold line and then make a second row of stitching ⅝″ away from the first. At the center front point, over the dividing line between the fourth and fifth pockets, you will need to make openings for the drawstring. Use an embroidery scissors to snip through only *one* layer of suede between the 2 rows of topstitching. Make a vertical slash approximately ½″ long, being very careful not to clip the stitches. Repeat this to make a second slash ½″ away from the first.

Tie drawstring. Fold the drawstring piece in half lengthwise with the right sides out. Topstitch ¼″ in from each edge. Trim the tie neatly to ⅛″ outside both

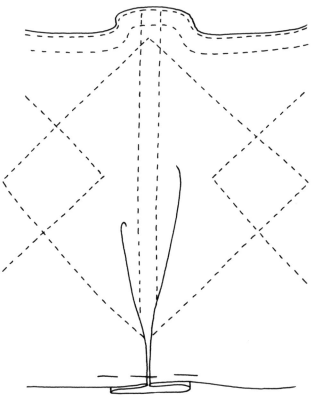

rows of stitching. Use a safety pin to insert the tie into one slash, through the top casing, and out the other slash. Pull the tie ends through the casing so they are even, insert the jar into the caddy, pull the drawstring snugly around the neck of the jar, and tie a bow.

▶ **HINT.** For nonsmokers, fill this jar with his favorite snack, such as candy or pretzels. The pockets are perfect for organizing pencils, rulers, pens, or small items at his desk.

Miniature Photo Hangings Everyone Can Do

Display 1, 2, or 3 miniature picture frames on a simple wall hanging made from felt or imitation suede.

MATERIALS:

¼ yard felt or imitation suede in brown, olive, or burgundy
¼ yard cord for hanging loop
4″ × 16″ cardboard rectangle
Three 2½″ round or square frames with rings for hanging
4¾″ piece ¼″ wooden dowel
2 wooden beads with a ¼″ hole in the center
½″ oval leather punch
White glue

DIRECTIONS:

Cutting. From the felt or suede cut one 8″ × 18″ rectangle. Cut one ½″ × 13″ lacing piece. Cut the 4″ × 16″ cardboard piece.

Assembly. The cardboard rectangle is used to back the 8″ × 18″ piece of felt or suede. Place the 8″ × 18″ piece on a flat surface. Center the 4″ × 16″ cardboard rectangle on top so that it is 2″ down from the top 8″ end. Fold the 18″ sides of the material over the cardboard and glue them in place. They will meet at the center back of the cardboard. Allow to dry thoroughly.

Frames. Put a picture in each frame. Turn the hanging over. Lightly draw a chalk line down the center of the hanging. Center the 3 frames on the right side. Place the top frame 3½″ from the top of the felt. Position the next 2 frames on the hanging so they are spaced about ½″ apart. Center them all on the chalk line. Make a chalk mark just inside the ring on top of each frame. Also make a mark ⅛″ outside each ring on top of the frame. Remove the frame and use the ½″ oval punch to cut a horizontal oval at each chalk mark. Center the slits over the center line of the hanging. Punch the openings as described under the Photo Album later in this chapter.

Insert the lacing strip through the first slit at the top of the hanging. Use the point of your scissors to coax it through if necessary. Pull it through to the front of the hanging so that only 1″ remains on the back side. Glue the 1″ section of the lacing strip to the back of the hanging and allow it to dry.

Insert the lacing strip through the ring of one frame from the front to the back. Pass the strip directly through the next slit to the back of the frame. Go to the next slit and push the lacing strip through to the front of the hanging. Attach the remain-

ing 2 frames in the same manner. Glue the end of the lacing strip to the back of the hanging.

On the back of the hanging center the wooden dowel under the 2″ extension at the top of the hanging. The dowel will extend ¼″ beyond each side. Fold the 2″ over the dowel and glue it in place. Allow it to dry. Glue one bead on each end of the dowel. Tie the cord to the dowel just inside each bead. Adjust the length as desired and tie a knot invisibly on the back side. Cut the cord ends off close to the knot.

The lower edge of the hanging is cut into a double-pointed end. Place a chalk mark on the center line of the hanging 2″ up from the bottom of the hanging. Draw a chalk line connecting this mark to each outer lower corner of the hanging, forming a triangle. Using a heavy scissors, cut through all thicknesses on the chalk lines.

▶ HINT. These framed collections of pictures are easy for kids to make. They can insert their own pictures and give them as perfect gifts for Grandfather's living room or Dad's office.

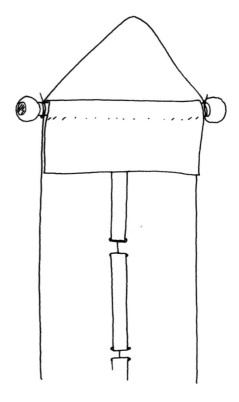

Simple Items Papered with Maps of Exciting Places

MATERIALS:

Accessory item with a smooth surface to cover, such as a wastecan, lampshade, or scrapbook

Heavy paper maps large enough to cover the accessory item—maps come in large sizes and are simple to cut and use to cover any smooth surface. There is a map to interest almost everyone. Choose from hiking, sailing, and biking maps or maps of roads, countries, and even stars.

Wallpaper paste

Narrow trim or braid for finishing edges (optional)

White glue

Clear shellac, lacquer, or varnish

DIRECTIONS:

Pattern. It is necessary to make a paper pattern of the surface to be covered before cutting into the map. Tape sheets of newspaper together to make a pattern and practice the method of covering. Wrap the paper around the object tightly and tape it in place. Draw lines on the paper to indicate where any cutting or seams should occur. Generally, allow the pattern to overlap for about 1″ at seams. Carefully remove the tape and flatten the pattern out. Cut the paper to custom fit the object you are covering. Refer to Chapter 2 for ideas on covering items with paper.

Cutting. Center the paper pattern on the map. Try to focus on the special area or town by placing it prominently on the object. Hold the pattern down flat on the map with one hand and draw around it with the other. Remove the pattern and cut it out on the lines.

Working on a newspaper-covered flat surface, apply wallpaper paste to the wrong side of the map, following the manufacturer's instructions carefully. Working quickly, glue the map to the object as you planned when making the pattern. Overlap seams where necessary. Remove excess glue around the edges with a soft dry cloth.

Trim. Use white glue to apply trim around the edges of the map. This serves as decoration and also conceals the cut edges of the map neatly. Select a ropelike or braided type of trim that is subtle and enhances the object well. Gold or natural colors look best. Cut the trim to fit around the object exactly. Dab a bit of white glue on the cut ends of the trim to prevent unraveling and glue the trim to the object, placing the butted ends at the back or least noticeable spot.

Finishing. Follow the manufacturer's instructions to apply one or more coats of

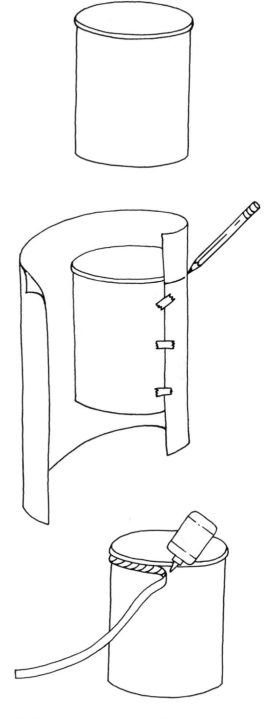

shellac, lacquer, or varnish to the map. This protects the paper from wear and tear and also allows it to be easily wiped clean.

▶ **HINT.** Cover a scrapbook or journal with a map of his favorite vacation spot. Mark the town and route traveled on the map and give them as a bon voyage gift.

Alma Mater Pillow to Crochet

MATERIALS:

1 large school emblem
½ yard 44″ or 54″ heavy blanket wool fabric in the darker school color
One 3½-ounce skein 4-ply yarn in the lighter school color
Size F crochet hook
Stuffing

DIRECTIONS:

Pillow front and back. Cut two 14″ squares from the wool fabric. Overcast the raw edges in matching thread to prevent raveling. Work a buttonhole stitch around the entire outer edge of each square as described under the crocheted Stadium Blanket in Chapter 3. Place 1 stitch every ¼″ so there are 56 stitches on each side. Work 3 stitches in each corner as described under the Stadium Blanket.

Crocheted Gusset. A 2″ crocheted gusset is inserted between the pillow front and back to give it a boxed shape. Make one gusset as follows:

Gauge: 4 sc = 1″   4 rows = 1″

With the light-colored yarn, ch 10 plus ch 1 to turn (11 sts).

Row 1: Insert the hook into the second chain from the hook, work 1 sc, work 1 sc in each ch across, ch 1, turn (10 sts).

Row 2: Insert the hook into the first stitch, work 1 sc in each st across, ch 1, turn (10 sts).

Rows 3–224: Repeat row 2. Fasten off after row 224. Knot end and sink yarn end into stitches invisibly. Block piece to 2″ × 56″, following manufacturer's instructions.

Assembly. Slip-stitch the first crochet row to the last row, forming a ring. Make sure it is not twisted. Working from the right side, join the gusset to the pillow front with slip stitches as described under the Stadium Blanket. With wrong sides together place the crocheted seam at the center bottom edge of the pillow. Place 56 single crochet stitches on each side of the pillow. Put 1 stitch in the corner.

Repeat this to join the pillow back. Work the stitches so they correspond to the stitches on the pillow front. Stop 6″ from the end. Stuff the pillow through the opening. Continue slip-stitching to close the opening. Secure the yarn end neatly. Hand-stitch the school emblem to the center of the pillow front.

► HINT. Use this pillow technique to finish any piece of needlepoint, cross-stitch, or embroidery. Work out a school emblem or family tree yourself to use as a pillow front. Also, many packaged needlework kits have appropriate designs for men that would look great made up in this style of pillow.

Easy Pillows to Make from Felt Pennants

MATERIALS:

1 printed felt pennant for each pillow
Felt remnant ½" larger than the pennant in a contrasting color
Thread to match the felt
Stuffing

DIRECTIONS:

Cutting. Cut a pillow back from the felt using the pennant as a pattern. If the pennant has felt streamers at the short end, baste them flat toward the center of the pennant so that they do not get cut. Center the pennant on the felt with the right side up. Pin the 2 layers together, leaving a 6″ opening in the center of the short end for stuffing. Unpin the pennant streamers so that they do not get caught in the stitching.

Assembly. Edgestitch the pennant to the felt, placing the stitches ⅛″ in from the edge of the pennant. Use a pinking shears to trim the excess felt backing away about ½″ beyond the stitched edges of the pennant.

Stuff the pillow through the opening at the short end, using a spoon to push the stuffing into the point and corners. Edgestitch the opening closed. Trim the backing felt off with a straight scissors so it is even with the short end of the pillow. Release the basted felt streamers.

If your pennant has no streamers, you can make them from the felt scraps. Cut five 1″-wide strips that measure 1″ longer than the short end of the pennant. Match the ends of 2 streamers and stitch one pair to the front of the pennant at the top and bottom corners of the pennant's short end. Topstitch the remaining strip to the short end of the pennant so it covers the matched ends of the streamers.

►**HINT.** Small pennants make terrific appliqués for the back of a jacket. Simply center the pennant on the back of the jacket and edgestitch it in place.

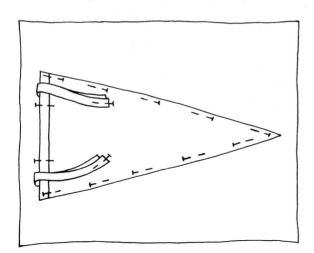

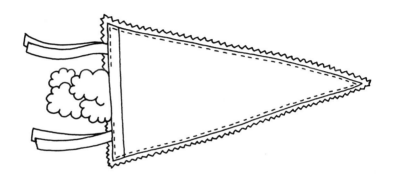

Photo Album to Decorate and Personalize in Punchwork

MATERIALS:

1 photo album 12″ × 14″ or slightly larger—select one with plain inverted hinged
   covers
½ yard 44″-wide dark green imitation suede
Heavy decorative or adhesive paper for lining—two 12″ × 14″ pieces
³⁄₃₂″ leather hole-punch tool
½ yard metallic gold adhesive paper
Kraft paper for a pattern 18″ × 22″
2½″ Gothic letter stencils
White glue

DIRECTIONS:

Pattern. Remove the front and back album covers. Put the pages and the screws aside so they won't get lost. Check to see if the front and back covers are identical in shape. If not, you will need to make a separate pattern for each.

Working flat, trace the cover outline (hinge included) onto the pattern paper. Mark the placement of the hinge fold line on the pattern. Mark the top edge of the pattern. Add 2½″ to all sides. Cut the pattern out.

The punched design is centered on the front cover. To position it, fold the hinge section of the pattern to the back along the fold line. Fold the 2½″ on the remaining 3 sides to the back. Next, fold the actual size pattern into quarters. Mark the horizontal and vertical centers with a crease. Open the pattern out flat.

One quarter of the design is given in the illustration. Transfer this to tracing paper. Transfer the design to each quarter of the album pattern, matching the center lines as indicated. Flip the pattern over to transfer it to the opposite sides.

Use the stencils to draw the desired initials on the baseline in the center of the cover pattern. Refer to the Basic Techniques for Using Letters in Chapter 1. Erase the stencil bridges in the letters so you have a simple outlined letter. Make sure to place them upright with the cover hinge on the left side. Mark dots around the letter outlines, spaced ¼″ apart. Each dot will become a ³⁄₃₂″ punched hole.

Punchwork. Use the paper pattern to cut a front and back cover from the suede. Center the pattern on the right side of the front cover piece. Working flat, use a stapler to secure the pattern to the cover

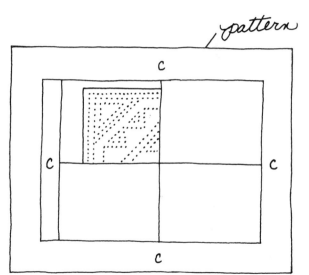

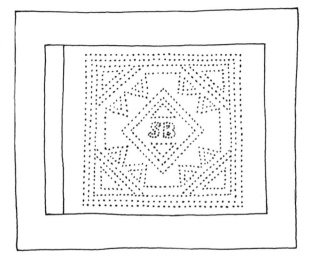

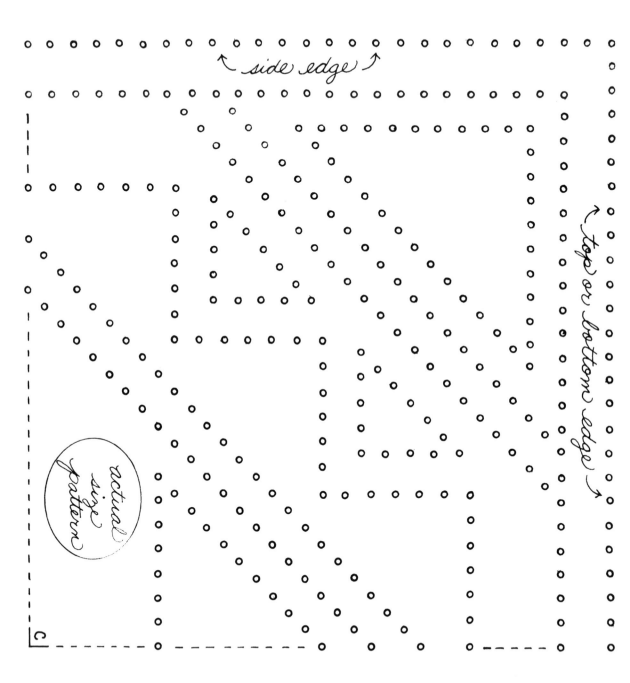

side edge

top or bottom edge

actual
size
pattern

C

around all outer edges. Use thick layers of newspaper or heavy cardboard underneath the cover to protect the work surface during punching.

Use a hammer and the ³⁄₃₂″ punch tool to punch the holes. Center the tool over each dot on the design and hit it with the hammer. Punch directly through the pattern and the suede at the same time. Punch out the entire design and the letters. Remove the staples and the pattern.

Assembly. Apply gold adhesive paper to the album so it will show through the punchwork cover. Measure the actual size of the front cover without the hinge. Subtract ½″ from the length and width. Cut one piece of gold adhesive paper to these dimensions. Remove the backing and center this on the album front cover.

With the wrong side up, place the punchwork cover on a flat surface. Center the album front, covered in gold, on top with the right side down. Fold the 2½″ suede edges to the inside of the album and tape in place. Turn the cover over to make sure that the design is centered on the front. Adjust and retape if necessary.

Fold the suede over the hinge section and carefully mark the placement for the holes on both sides. Punch the holes. Fold and glue each suede corner over the album cover, mitering them as described under the Paper Portfolio in Chapter 2. Glue all the suede edges down to the inside cover of the album. Repeat this on the album back.

The lining paper is glued to the inside covers to hide the edges. Center it so one edge is aligned with the hinge fold line. Reassemble the album covers and pages.

►HINT. Use this design to cover all sorts of books. It would make a great stamp collector's album, scrapbook, or even a baby book for a fine newborn son.

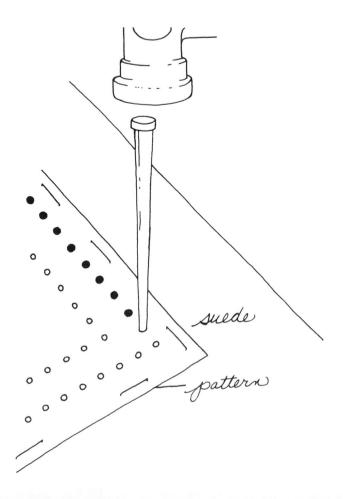

suede

pattern

7.

Make It for Home Sweet Home

PROJECT

Quick Pillows Made from Dyed Handkerchieves

MATERIALS:
1 white handkerchief with a plaid border for each pillow
2½ yards 2″-wide bias hem facing in a contrasting color
1 package fabric dye in a dark color
½ yard fleece
½ yard fabric for the pillow back
Thread to match the hem facing
Stuffing

DIRECTIONS:

Dying. The white handkerchieves with plaid borders are easy to dye any color. The plaid design becomes more subtle when dyed. Follow the manufacturer's instructions to prepare the dye solution, except use only one half the amount of water specified. Dye all the handkerchieves at the same time, making sure to stir them continuously. Wash, dry, and press the handkerchieves after they are dyed.

Quilting. Use the handkerchief as a pattern to cut one square from the fleece and the fabric. With the right side up, baste the handkerchief to the fleece around the entire outer edge. Baste an X of stitching across the handkerchief to keep it from shifting during quilting. Hand- or machine-quilt along the lines of the plaid border.

Assembly. Each corner of the handkerchief is rounded. Place a coffee cup so it is aligned with one corner. Draw around it and cut on the line. Repeat this on the remaining corners.

With wrong sides together, match the pillow front to the back. Trim the back to match the rounded corners of the front. Baste them together ½" from the outer edges. Leave a 6" opening in the center of one side for stuffing. Stuff the pillow and baste the opening closed.

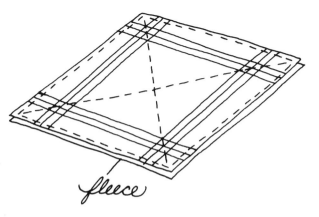

fleece

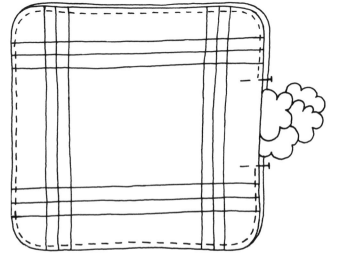

Binding. Apply the hem facing to the outer edges of the pillow using a ¾" seam allowance. Follow the instructions given under Racket Covers in Chapter 4 for applying bias binding. Begin applying the bias on the right side of the pillow, easing it around the curved corners. Press under ½" and overlap the ends neatly where they meet. Wrap the bias to the back of the pillow over the ¾" seam allowance, forming the look of extra-thick piping. Machine-finish the binding by stitching in the well of the seam from the front of the pillow.

► **HINT.** Use this method to make over-size pillows from bandanas. Elaborate-looking quilted effects are easy to do by simply quilting around the printed bandana designs.

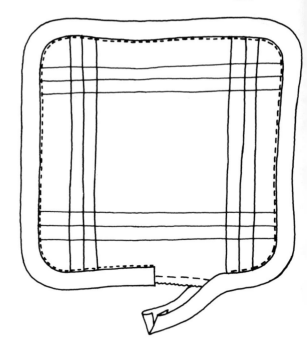

Comforter to Fashion from Old Shirts

MATERIALS:

17 shirts in assorted colors
4½ yards light blue broadcloth for backing
Two 72″ × 72″ rolls of quilt batting
Light blue thread
9 yards 1″-wide light blue bias tape
1 ball lightweight crochet cotton in a coordinating color

DIRECTIONS:

If you haven't got 17 shirts on hand, a good assortment can often be found very inexpensively at flea markets and used clothing stores.

Cutting. Cut the shirts apart along the seams of the shirt so the fabric can be spread out flat. Cut the patchwork squares so the straight sides of the squares correspond to the fabric grain. Cut one 13" × 13" square from the back of each shirt. Cut twenty 7" × 7" squares from the shirt fronts. Use the remaining fabric and sleeves to cut 324 squares 4" × 4".

Patchwork Top. Follow the illustration to lay out the fabric squares for the patchwork. Arrange the colors in the way you feel looks best. Begin at the center and work outward. Seam the squares together into rows first and then seam the rows in place. Press the seams open.

Beginning at the center, seam 2 rows of 4 small squares to the opposite sides of 1 large square. Join 2 rows of 8 small squares to the remaining sides of the large center square. Match all the seam lines of the squares where they intersect each other.

Next join 1 row of 4 medium squares to opposite sides of the patchwork. Seam 1 row of 6 medium squares to the remaining

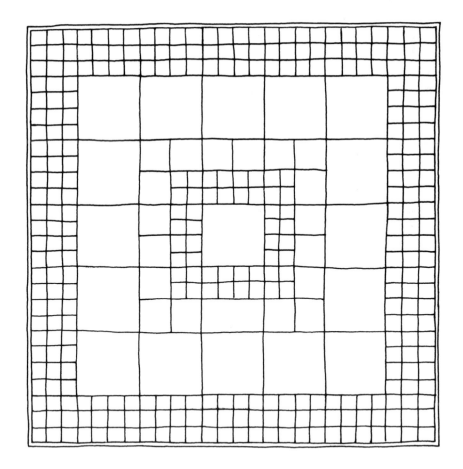

□ — 4"× 4"

▢ — 7"× 7"

▢ — 13" × 13"

opposite sides. Make 2 rows of 3 large squares and stitch them to opposite sides of the patchwork. Stitch 1 row of 5 large squares to the other 2 sides. For the outer border sew 3 rows of 20 small squares to opposite sides of the comforter. Join 3 rows of 26 small squares to each of the last 2 sides.

Quilt Backing. Fold the 4½ yard piece of backing fabric in half crosswise. Cut it in half along the fold line so you have two 2¼ yard pieces. With right sides together, seam them together to make one piece that is slightly larger than the patchwork top. On one side, with right sides together, place the long edge of each piece together and machine stitch. Make ¼ " clips in the selvage edges every 2 " and press the seam open. This seam will be centered on the back of the comforter.

Quilt Assembly. A comforter is filled with more than one layer of batting. It is thicker and more puffed looking than a quilt. The layers of a comforter are held together by tufting with cotton crochet yarn. If you prefer to quilt the patchwork rather than tuft it, use only one layer of batting and hand- or machine-stitch on top of all the seam lines. Secure all the thread ends where you stop stitching.

The patchwork top, batting, and backing fabric are joined by smoothing each layer out on top of one another. Enlist the help of a friend to spread the layers out flat. It is a bit tricky to do by yourself.

Clear a place on the floor that is large enough to spread the quilt out flat. Take your shoes off because you will need to step on the quilt. Try not to work on a rug if possible. With the wrong side up, put the seamed backing piece on the floor first. Straighten it out until it lies perfectly flat. Weight the corners down with inverted coffee cups or canned goods. This keeps you from disturbing the backing fabric as you put the next layer in place. Open the roll of batting and unfold all the creases. It helps

to shake and fluff it gently. Stand facing your helper on opposite sides of the quilt. Carefully straighten out the batting and lower it onto the backing piece.

Smooth out any bumps or unevenness in the batting. Weight it down on each corner. The batting should lie completely flat on the backing piece. If you are making a comforter, use more than one layer of batting, spreading additional layers out in the same manner. Match the outer edges of all the layers of batting to the raw edge of the backing fabric and trim them off evenly. Baste them together.

Lower the patchwork top, with the right side up, on top of the batting. Be careful not to disturb the smoothed-out batting. Make sure it is absolutely flat. Remove any wrinkles by lifting and gently adjusting the corners and edges.

When you are certain that all 3 layers are flat and smooth, pin them together. Begin in the center of the quilt. Pin through all thicknesses in radiating lines from the center point of the quilt. Baste the layers together along the pin lines. Begin basting at the center and work outward. Keep the quilt as flat on the floor as possible during the basting. Baste the raw edge of the quilt top to the batting and the backing on all sides.

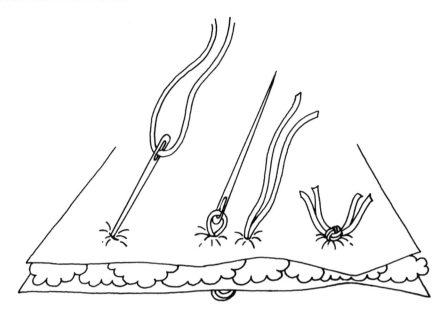

Tufting. This is a quick way to tie all the layers together to make a wonderful, thick comforter. Yarn can be used for tufting; however, the best material to use is a fine cotton cord such as that used for crocheted doilies. It comes in lots of colors. One tuft is made at the corner of each patchwork square.

The tufting keeps the layers of batting from snarling up inside the comforter. The more tufting you do the more firm the comforter will be. Often, during use or laundering, the batting will lump up inside if it is not tufted sufficiently. Place a pin through all layers in each spot where a tuft will be placed. Turn the comforter over and check to make sure that the backing fabric is smoothed out evenly and there are no pleats formed by the pinned tufts.

Use heavy thread, yarn, or crochet cotton. Thread a piece about 12″ long in a large-eyed needle. Holding the needle vertically, insert it through all the layers. Pull the thread through until about a 4″ end remains. Take a ⅛″ or ¼″ stitch on the bottom layer, and insert the needle vertically up through all the layers. Be careful not to let the 4″ end of the thread slip through the fabric.

Insert the needle down again at the first spot next to the 4″ end. Pull the thread through to the underside. This security stitch should squeeze the 3 layers together snugly. Return the thread to the top as you did before.

Pull the two ends gently. Tie a square knot closely against the fabric. Clip the thread ends to about ½″ to 1″ long. Repeat this on all corners, working from the center outward.

Binding. After the comforter is completely tufted, trim the outer edges so all 3 layers are even and straight. Bind the edge with the 1″-wide bias tape as described under the Racket Cover.

▶ **Hint.** A fabulous wool throw can be made using wool scraps for the patchwork. Omit the batting and back the patchwork with an old blanket. Tuft the patchwork to the blanket and fringe all the outside raw edges as a perfect finish.

Picture Frames to Weave with Newspaper Strips

MATERIALS:

1 plain wooden frame that is flat on the front side (or wooden stretcher strips
  joined to make a frame)
Newspaper
White glue
Lacquer, shellac, or varnish in clear or colored high-gloss finish
Staple gun and staples (for wood)
Stapler and staples (for paper)

DIRECTIONS:

Cutting. Cut the newspaper into ½" or 1" strips. Open out 6 to 8 layers of newspaper and place them on a flat surface. The strips are easier to work with when they are absolutely flat. Press them with a warm iron to remove all creases. Use a yardstick and felt tip pen to draw the strips on the top layer of newspaper. Draw the strips so they run across the longest direction of the newspaper. The side that you draw the lines on becomes the *wrong* side of the weaving so that the lines do not show. Make sure the strips are uniform in width so that the weaving will not be distorted by uneven strips.

After you have drawn the lines, make sure that all the layers are smoothed out flat. With the paper stapler, place one staple at both ends of all the strips, securing all the layers together. Working flat, cut the layered strips out on the drawn lines. Place the cut strips aside on a flat surface so they do not become wrinkled or tangled. Cut one full page of strips and then cut more as you need them.

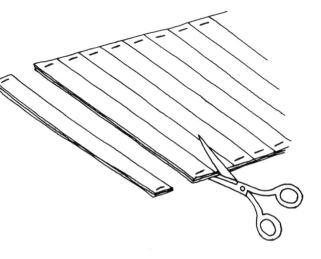

Weaving. Measure the width of your frame and add 5". This is the width of the finished woven piece needed to cover the frame. Lay enough strips out next to each other to equal this measurement. The drawn lines on the strips should all face upward. Place the ends of the strips even with the work surface and tape them down for easier weaving. These vertical strips are called the warp strips.

Beginning at one side, weave one newspaper strip horizontally across the entire row of warp strips. Weaving in this direction is called the weft. Pass the weft strip alternately over and under the warp strips. Make certain that during weaving you pick up all the layers of each newspaper strip. The warp and weft strips must be perpendicular to each other. The woven

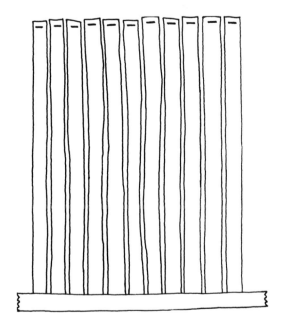

piece should be a perfect rectangle. After
you finish weaving each strip, make sure
it is straight and packed tightly against the
previous row. Gently lift the weaving and
staple the weft strip to the outermost warp
strip on both sides. This secures the strip
in place.

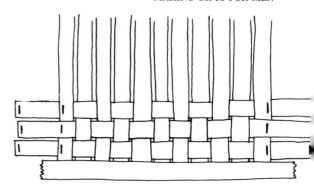

You will need to weave a piece 5″ to 6″
larger than the frame that you are covering. This will provide the extra weaving
necessary to wrap around the sides and
back of the frame. Continue weaving until you have a rectangular piece that extends
2″ to 3″ beyond the frame on all sides.

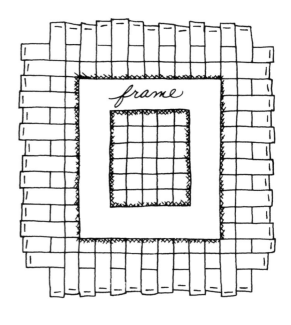

Covering the Frame. Remove the glass
and all backing from the frame. Spread glue
on the front of the frame. Center the glued
side on the woven piece. Align the outer
edges of the frame with the woven strips
on all sides as best as possible. Allow the
glue to dry thoroughly.

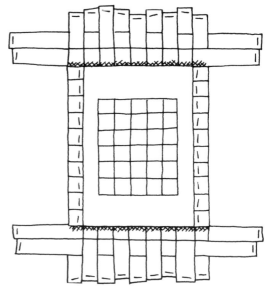

The sides of the woven paper are
wrapped around to the back of the frame
and stapled in place. Apply a small amount
of glue to one side of the frame. Fold the
weaving tightly around the side and staple
the middle strip to the back of the frame.
Pull the weaving snugly around the frame
and continue stapling each strip to the back
of the frame until you reach one corner.
Repeat this in the other direction until one
side is completely stapled down. Trim off
all the excess woven paper next to the
staples. Some unweaving will naturally occur at the corner when you cut. Remove
all loose strips. Restaple the weaving
together carefully if necessary.

Corners. Wrap the ends of the woven strips around the side of the frame for about 1 " at the corner. Trim off the excess. Glue the ends flat to the side of the frame. Take your time so that the corners are covered neatly. Fold up the adjacent side of the weaving and staple it to the back of the frame as you did before. Trim off the excess woven ends at the corner. Reconstruct the woven look by snipping the strips off even with the intersection of an adjoining strip and gluing all the layers flat in place. Cover the remaining sides and corners of the frame in the same manner.

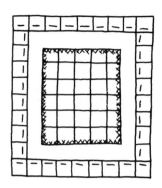

Inside Corners. Draw lines around the inner openings of the frame that are 2 " inside each side of the wooden frame. Use a knife to cut this ''window'' from the center of the weaving. Draw a line from the corner of the window to the inside corner of the frame. Cut on these lines. Remove all loose strips. Glue and staple the remaining strips to the back of the frame as you did before. Glue down the small cut ends at each inside corner. Trim and glue the inner edges as flat as possible so the glass will fit back into the frame.

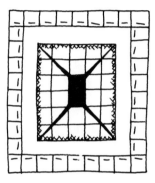

Finishing. Apply several coats of lacquer, shellac, or varnish to the front and sides of the covered frame. Follow the manufacturer's instructions carefully. Tinted finishes will add color but still allow the newspaper print to show through. The frames can also be painted if you prefer. Cut a photograph to fit the frame and reassemble the frame with the glass and the backing.

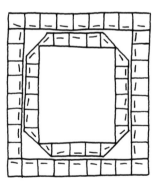

▶ **HINT.** Use this technique to cover almost any smooth, straight surface. Decorate a straight lampshade or wastebasket for a perfect office accessory.

Beach Chair with Stenciled "Parking Spot"

MATERIALS:

1 sling-style beach chair
Gray canvas—measure the length of the chair seat to determine yardage
   needed (44″-wide fabric includes enough for a pillow)
⅛ yard 1″-wide Velcro
Bright yellow acrylic paint in a small tube
Small stencil brush
2″ Gothic letter stencils
Gray thread
Stuffing for the pillow

DIRECTIONS:

Pattern. Remove the original cover from the chair, making notes on how to reassemble it. Remove all the stitching from the chair cover and press it flat. Use this as a pattern to cut out the new gray cover. Use the old cover as a guide for hemming and assembling the new one. Hem the sides and make casings as needed at the top and bottom edges. For the pillow cut 2 rectangles 12 " × 16 ". Also cut two 2 " × 9 " pieces for straps.

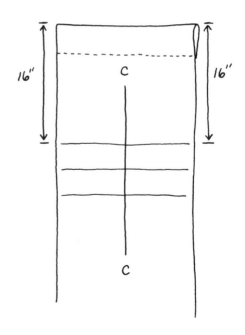

Placement. Mark the top edge of the new chair cover. Beginning at the top edge, measure 16 " down on each side and make marks on the right side of the fabric. Use chalk to draw a line across the cover at the 16 " point. Draw 2 more lines below and parallel to the first one, all spaced 3 " apart.

On the right side, measure 5½ " down from one long edge of one of the pillow pieces. Draw a line that is parallel to the long edge. Draw a second line 3 " below the first. All these lines are the baselines for the lettering. Refer to Basic Techniques for Using Letters in Chapter 1.

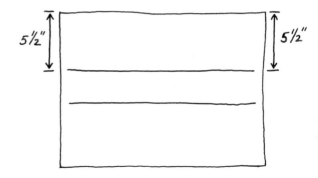

Fold the chair cover and one pillow piece in half lengthwise. Crease along the fold line and mark the vertical center of each with chalk. This line will intersect the baselines perpendicularly. The words ''No Parking'' are placed in two lines on the pillow. ''Reserved for [insert name]'' goes on the chair seat in 3 lines.

Count the number of letters and spaces in each line. Begin with the center letter. Use the stencil to outline the letter in chalk. Work outward to the left and right, outlining each letter. Outline all the letters on the pillow and chair cover in chalk. Check for accuracy before you stencil the letters.

Stenciling. Cover a hard, flat working surface with newspaper. Spread the chair and pillow covers out so you will be stenciling the letters in an upright position. Squeeze a small amount of paint onto a saucer. Use the chalk outlines to position the corresponding letter stencil. Begin at the top row. Lightly dip the brush into the paint on the saucer. Dab the brush up and down on a bare spot on the saucer. This will distribute a small amount of paint evenly on the stencil brush. Always work with a very dry brush. Test a few stenciled letters on scrap paper before working on the canvas.

Hold the edges of the stencil flat against the canvas as you work. Dab the color onto the letter with quick up and down movements, always holding the brush vertically. Cover the letter with an even coat of paint so the edges look crisp and clean. Work consistently so the color is solid and opaque. After each letter is completed, carefully lift the stencil off vertically to prevent smudges. Allow the letters to dry to the touch before proceeding.

Use paper and masking tape to mask out the previously stenciled areas as you continue. This prevents any stray paint splatters from getting on the canvas.

When you are stenciling on a dark color such as gray, a second coat may be needed to make the color look really bright. If you feel this is necessary, stencil the letters again in the same manner as before.

Pillow. Make the straps that hold the pillow in position first. Overcast the 2 long edges of each piece with zigzag stitches. Press ½ " to the wrong side of the fabric along both of the overcast edges. Topstitch ¼ " from each folded edge.

Cut the Velcro into two 2¼ " pieces. Pull the 2 sides of the Velcro apart so you have a hooked side and a fuzzy side. Topstitch the fuzzy sides to the right side of the plain pillow back. Position them vertically so they are 1¾ " in from the shorter sides of the pillow back and 1½ " down from the long top edge.

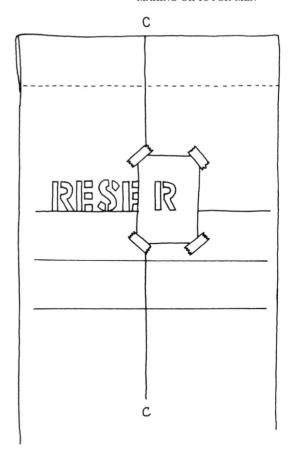

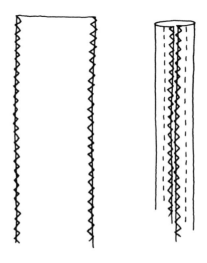

Pin the plain end of each strap to the top edge of the pillow back. Place the wrong side of the strap against the right side of the back. Position them 1¾" in from the side edges. Baste them in place. Tack the free ends of the straps to the center of the pillow back so they don't get caught in the stitching.

With right sides together and both top edges up, pin the pillow front to the back. Match the outer raw edges and corners. Machine straight stitch 3 sides and 4 corners, leaving a 6" opening in the center of the bottom edge for stuffing.

Stitch darts in each corner to make the pillow into a boxed shape. Near one corner grasp the pillow front with one hand and the back with the other. Pull them apart as far as possible and lay the corner down flat. Press the seam allowances open. Make sure the adjacent seams lie on top of one another.

Draw a line that is perpendicular to the seam 1" down from the point at the corner. Baste, then stitch on this line through all thicknesses. Repeat this on the other 3 corners.

Turn the pillow right side out through the opening. Stuff and hand slip-stitch the opening closed. Install the new canvas seat on the chair. Wrap the straps around the rod at the top of the chair so the pillow is positioned correctly. The ends of the straps should overlap the Velcro on the pillow back. Trim them down if necessary. Overcast the short raw end of each strap. Topstitch the hooked side of each Velcro piece to the wrong side of the strap end. Attach the pillow and Velcro the strap in place.

► HINT. For the indoorsman, stencil the Parking Spot design on a canvas director's chair for the office or family room. You may find that you need to make one for each family member.

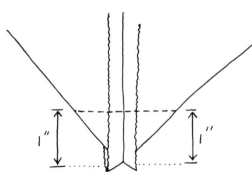

First Aid Kit to Put Together and Paint

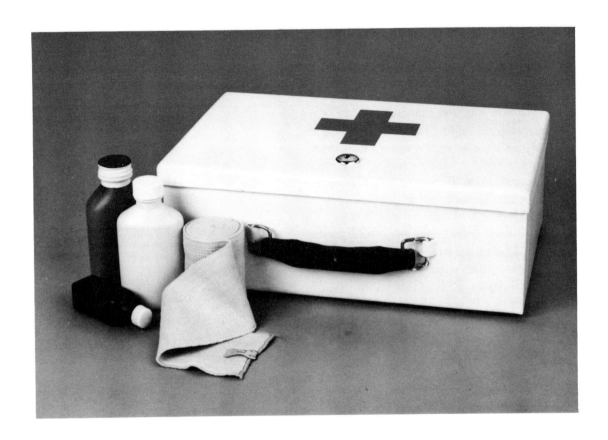

MATERIALS:

1 metal security or file box approximately 4″H × 12″W × 8″D
White and red spray enamel
Suggested kit ingredients: Gauze, bandages, smelling salts, ointments, elastic
  bandage, adhesive tape, aspirin, alcohol, cotton, Mercurochrome.

DIRECTIONS:

Painting. Paint the box exterior white first. Areas that you do not want to paint white, such as the metal lock, latch, and handle, must be covered. Use masking tape to mask out small areas. For best results, cut the tape to match the shape of whatever you are covering. Wrap a small piece of newspaper around the handle and secure it with tape. Any parts of the box that are not covered will get sprayed white.

NOTE. If you would rather not spray paint the box, use a small brush and a can of enamel. Eliminate covering the metal parts and carefully paint around all locks, latches, and handles.

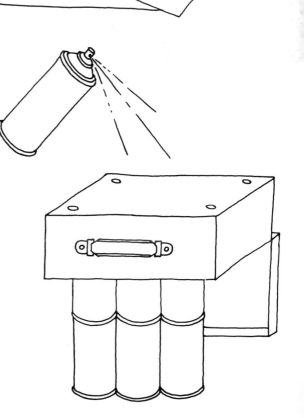

If your box has an overlapping lid, it is necessary to paint this first. Open the lid and place a piece of newspaper under it to prevent any stray paint from getting inside the box. Close the lid over the paper and paint it, following the manufacturer's instructions. Allow it to dry thoroughly.

The rest of the box is painted upside down. Stack 2 or 3 layers of full soda cans on top of each other for a support. Open the lid and place the inside of the box on top of the cans. Make sure it is well balanced and secure. Cover the already-painted lid with newspaper taped to the inside. Paint the entire box bottom section and hinge area as you did before.

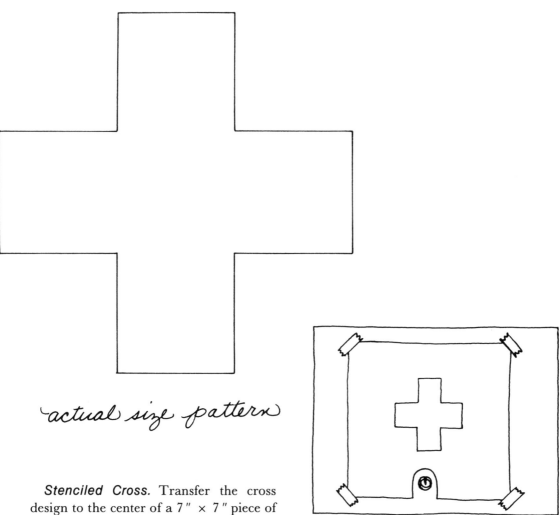

actual size pattern

Stenciled Cross. Transfer the cross design to the center of a 7″ × 7″ piece of cardboard. Use a paper knife to cut it out. Lightly mark the placement of the cross on the box lid, using the stencil. Keep it spaced several inches away from locks, latches, or handles. Center it as much as possible. The crossbars of the cross should be parallel with the edges of the lid.

Place the stencil over the marked placement lines. It should lay flat on the lid. Cut away areas of the stencil to avoid locks, etc. Use tiny pieces of masking tape to hold it in place. Cover the box around the stencil with newspaper and tape so no stray red paint will spoil the bright white finish. Paint the cross red.

The words "First Aid" can be added to the lid if there's room. Use 1″ Roman letter stencils and follow the stenciling instructions given under the Beach Chair. Center the letters and position them where they look best on the box. If you are using spray paint for the stencils, remember to carefully block out all white areas that are not being sprayed.

Note. If you are using regular paint, use a stencil brush and follow the stenciling instructions given under the Beach Chair.

Filling. Arrange the first aid materials inside the box so they are easily seen. Make a list of your local emergency telephone numbers and tape it inside the lid.

► **Hint.** Make a soft, lightweight first aid kit for campers and backpackers. Use the red cross pattern as an appliqué pattern. Stitch up the Zippered Shaving Kit in Chapter 8 in white with the red fabric cross appliquéd to one side.

Lampshade Handstitched from Old Ties

MATERIALS:
16 to 20 old ties (depending on the size of the lampshade)
1 lampshade with hanging lamp assembly
Black thread
2½ yards ½"-wide white bias tape
Glue

DIRECTIONS:

Pattern. Wrap a piece of newspaper around the lampshade to make a pattern. If the shade is quite large, tape several pieces of newspaper together until you make a large enough piece. Begin by taping a straight edge of the newspaper to the seam of the lampshade. Wrap the paper around the shade until it is completely covered. End at the seam where you started and trim the paper so it meets exactly at

the seam. Tape the paper seam to the shade. Trim the paper off at the top and bottom edges of the shade so it is exactly the same size and shape as the lampshade. Carefully remove the tape and the pattern. Fold the pattern in half, matching the 2 short straight edges to determine the vertical center of the lampshade cover. Mark the fold line.

Cover Assembly. Remove the point off of each tie by cutting straight across the *wider* end of the tie. Measure the height of the lampshade pattern and add 4″. This is the length that you will need to cut from each tie. Measure and mark this distance up from the straight cut end. Cut the tie off at the mark. Repeat on all the ties.

Carefully open the back seam of each cut tie and remove the linings and interfacings.

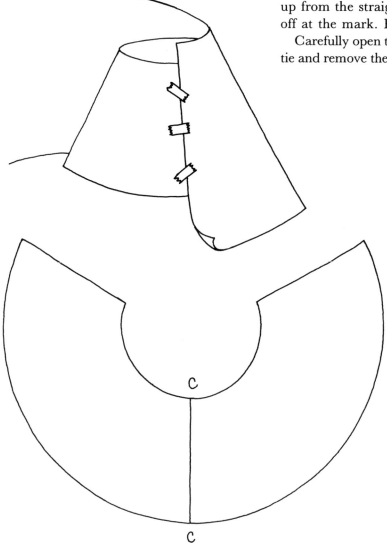

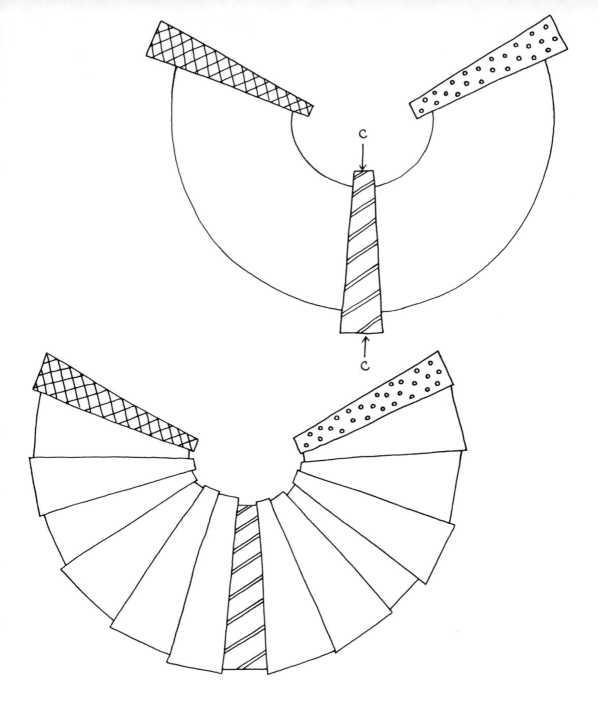

Lay the lampshade pattern out on a flat surface. Lay the ties out on the pattern. Put one tie at each seam edge and one over the center crease line. Pin the ties to the pattern so that the widest part is placed at the bottom of the pattern. The ties should extend equally at least 1″ above and below the edge of the pattern.

Add more ties to the pattern by laying them next to one another. They should cover the pattern so they radiate in an even manner from the top of the shade to the bottom. Fill the pattern with ties so they touch each other at the top of the pattern. The bottom of the pattern will probably be much wider than the ties can cover. Flare the bottom of each tie out to fill in the bottom edges of the pattern. Cover the pattern with ties completely and pin them to the pattern. Lightly steam them in position.

Join the ties by slip-stitching the pressed edges together invisibly. After all the ties are stitched together, trim the raw edges at the top and bottom curved edges so the ties extend evenly 1 ″ beyond the pattern. Remove the pattern and trim the tie seam allowances on the wrong side down to ½ ″. Press all seam allowances open.

Finishing. Pin the bias tape to the top curved edge of the cover so it overlaps the raw ends of the ties on the right side by ¼ ″. Repeat this on the bottom curved edge.

Wrap the cover around the lampshade. It should fit snugly but not tightly. Turn under the seam allowance on one tie where the cover will be seamed. Pin it in place and slip-stitch the cover closed.

Fold the cover to the inside at the top and bottom edges of the lampshade. Cut slits in the top of the cover to fit around the wire frame of the lamp as necessary. Fold it around the edge of the lampshade snugly. Use tape to hold it in place while you are working. Apply a small amount of glue to the wrong side of a short length of bias tape.

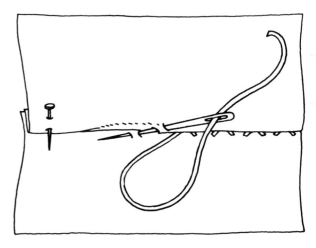

Press it in against the wrong side of the lampshade and retape it in place. Repeat this around the top and bottom edges of the lampshade. Allow it to dry thoroughly and remove all the tape. Attach the shade to the lamp assembly.

► **HINT.** If you can't locate enough old ties to cover the shade, visit your local used clothing store. They should have a big assortment of ties available very cheaply.

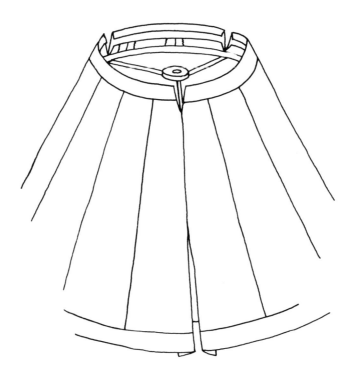

8.

Make It to Get Organized

PROJECT

Travel Bags to Sew in Three Sizes

MATERIALS:

(Changes for medium and large bags are given in parentheses)
⅛ (¼, ¼) yard prequilted fabric
¼ (⅜, ½) yard plain broadcloth in a coordinating color
1 (1½, 2) yards drawstring cord in a contrasting color
¼ (½, ¾) yards ½″-wide flat middy braid
Thread to match the broadcloth

DIRECTIONS:

One set of bags will organize all the loose
items that normally are packed into a suit-
case. The large bag easily accommodates
a pair of shoes. The medium bag is ideal
for holding socks, handkerchieves, and ties.
The small size is perfect for jewelry or tiny
items that might get lost easily.

Cutting. From the prequilted fabric, cut
two 3½″ × 5″ (6″ × 9″, 7½″ × 13″)
bottom pieces. From the broadcloth, cut
two 5″ × 5½″ (9″ × 9½″, 13″ × 13½″)
top pieces.

Assembly. The top and bottom sections
are assembled separately and then seamed
together.

With the right sides together, stitch the
2 bottom pieces together along the side and
bottom edges. Leave the top 5″ (9″, 13″)
end unsewn. Press the seams open. Overcast the edges. Darts are made at the bottom edge to form the corners of the bag.
Make the darted corners as described under
the Beach Chair in Chapter 7. The dart
stitching line is marked ¾″ (1¾″, 2¾″)
from the point. Trim the excess away ¼″
outside of the stitching line and overcast the
seam. Repeat this to make the other bag
corner.

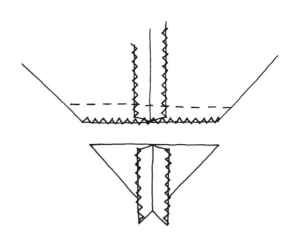

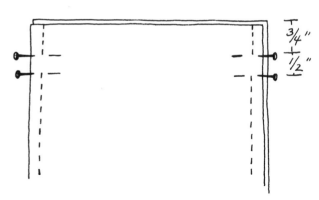

The top pieces are seamed right sides
together at the side seams. Seam the 5½″
(9½″, 13½″) edges, leaving a ½″ casing
opening at a point that is ¾″ down from
the top edge. The opening is for the insertion of the drawstring. Press the seams open
and then overcast.

A casing is made at the top for the
drawstring. Press under ¼″ at the top
edge. Press under ½″ and edgestitch the
casing in place along the inner pressed
edge.

Cut a piece of middy braid that is 9″ (17″, 25″) long. Seam the short ends together. With the right sides together, baste the braid to the bottom edge of the top section by matching the edge of the braid to the edge of the fabric. Have the braid seam at one side seam of the bag. Use a ¼″ seam allowance.

With right sides together, stitch the top to the bottom by matching the remaining raw edges. Be sure the side seams match. Use a ¼″ seam allowance. Overcast the edges together. Press the seam toward the top of the bag.

Cut the cord in half. Insert a safety pin into one end of the cording. Thread it through the casing entering and exiting at the ½″ opening in the seam. Knot both ends of the cording together. Repeat with the other piece of cord and the opening in the other side seam.

► **HINT.** These bags are terrific for organizing small items. Make the medium one to hold the chess, checker, or backgammon pieces described in Chapter 4.

TV Watcher's Caddy Made from Vinyl

MATERIALS:

¾ yard vinyl (main color)
¼ yard vinyl (contrast color)
Thread to match main color

DIRECTIONS:

Cutting. The caddy is designed to hang over the arm of his favorite chair. To determine the length of the base piece, measure the chair from the top of the arm to a point approximately 6″ to 8″ under the chair cushion. To this measurement add 18″ for the TV Caddy.

From the main color of vinyl, cut one base piece 15″ wide × the base piece length previously determined. Also cut one back pocket piece 10″ × 15″ and one front pocket piece 6″ × 15″. From the contrasting color, cut 3 binding strips 1½″ × 15″ and 2 binding strips that are 1½″ wide and as long as the base piece plus ½″ seam allowance.

Pockets. The top edges of the pockets are bound with the contrasting color. With right sides together, match one long edge of a short binding strip to one long edge of a pocket. Stitch, using a ⅜″ seam allowance. Wrap the binding strip to the back of the pocket piece. Tape the binding in place on the wrong side of the pocket. Working from the right side, stitch in the ''well'' of the seam formed by the binding. Remove the tape from the wrong side and trim the excess binding ¼″ away from the stitching line. Repeat for the second pocket piece.

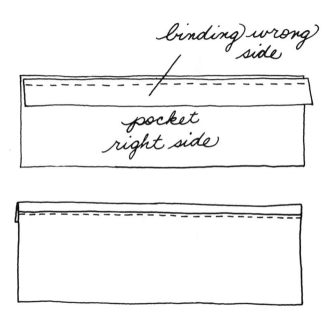

Using a white pencil, mark the 3 pocket division stitching lines on the right side of the front pocket. Beginning at the left side, the pocket widths are 3¾″, 3¾″, 4″, and 3½″.

The second 3¾″ pocket is for a small tissue pack. A 3½″ long slit is made vertically in the center of the pocket. To prevent the slit from tearing, use a hole punch to punch a hole at both ends of the slit.

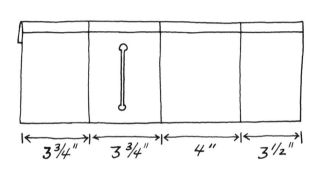

Baste the front pocket to the back pocket, matching the side and bottom edges. Stitch through both thicknesses on the stitching line. Follow the directions for stitching described under the Denim Work Apron, leaving a ⅛" space between the two rows of stitching.

Mark the pocket division on the back pocket piece. Measure 6½" in from left edge. Draw a line from the top of the back pocket to the top of the front pocket.

Baste the pocket section to the base piece, matching the sides and one short end. Stitch through all thicknesses on the back pocket stitching line as before. Stitch from the binding of the front pocket to the binding of the back pocket.

Finishing. Use the remaining short binding strip to bind the bottom edge of the caddy, encasing the pocket edges. Bind the long side edges. Turn under ½" of the side binding strip at the bottom bound edges. The remaining short end is left unbound so it does not cause a bump in your seat.

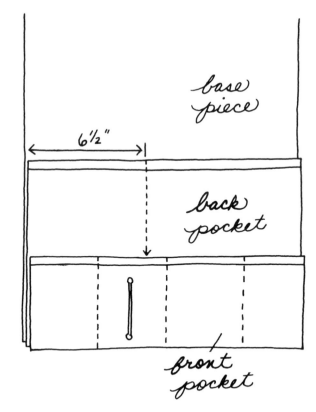

▶ **HINT.** Make this caddy up in heavy felt to use as a bedside organizer. Put the end of the base piece between the mattress and box springs so the pockets are within reach.

Laundry Bag for Sorting Light and Dark

MATERIALS:
1⅛ yards brown fabric
1¼ yards tan fabric
2 yards heavy cord
4″ Roman letter stencils
Thread to match both fabrics
Fabric fuser
½ yard interfacing
15 large grommets

DIRECTIONS:

Cutting. From the tan fabric, cut one
26″ × 40″ side piece and one 17″ × 35″
divider piece. From the brown fabric, cut
one 26″ × 40″ side piece and one 17″ circle for the bottom. To make the circle pattern, draw around your largest pan lid and
then extend the circle to the desired
diameter with a ruler. Also cut out a 17″
circle from the interfacing.

Lettering. Follow directions under
Machine Appliquéd Letters in Chapter 1.
Use the brown fabric to cut out the letters
for ''Light'' and the tan fabric for the
''Dark'' letters. The thread color should
match the letter color.

Position the letters as follows. ''Light''
is placed on the bottom left of the tan side
piece. ''Dark'' is on the bottom right of the
brown side piece. Start at the bottom edge
with the last letter in the word. Lightly draw
a line 5½″ in from the raw edge. The
center of the letters is placed on this line.
The bottom edge of the first letter is 4″ up
from the bottom edge. There is a ⅝″
space between the letters.

Assembly. Baste the interfacing to the
wrong side of the brown circle, matching
all raw edges. Fold the circle in half and
crease with your iron.

Both 17″ edges of the divider piece are
hemmed. Turn under ¼″ twice and edgestitch along the inner folded edge.

The wrong side of the brown side piece
is basted to the divider along the long side
edges. The bottom hem of the divider is
½″ above the bottom raw edge of the side
piece.

Pin the right side of the tan side piece
to the right side of the brown side piece.
Stitch, catching the divider in the seam.
Trim the seams to ¼″ and overcast.

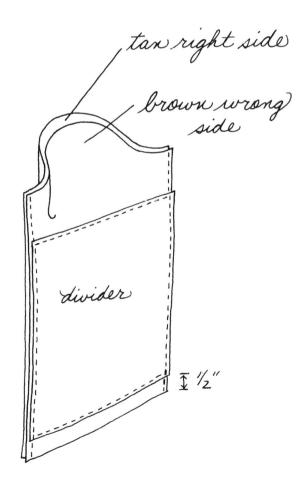

tan right side

brown wrong side

divider

½″

Divide the bag into quarters by folding the bottom edge in half, matching the seams. Mark the folds. Fold the circle into quarters and mark the folds. Seam the brown circle to the bag bottom, matching the quarter marks on the circle to the quarter marks on the bag. The crease line on the circle should be matched to the side seams of the bag. Trim the seams to ¼" and overcast.

Turn the bag right side out. The divider is now inside the bag. Match the bottom edge of the divider to the crease line on the bottom of the bag and hand-stitch in place.

Finishing. Overcast the top raw edges of the bag. Press a 2½" hem to the wrong side. Machine stitch the facing to the bag 2" from the folded edge.

Divide the top of the bag into 15 equal 3½" spaces. Make a mark 1" down from the top edge every 3½". Center a grommet over each mark, as described under the Denim Work Apron in Chapter 5. Insert cord in grommets, entering and exiting at the same point. Knot both ends together.

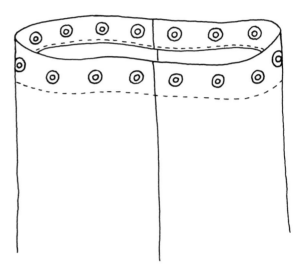

▶ **HINT.** This giant drawstring bag is ideal for storing almost anything. Omit the divider piece and make it to transport sports equipment or camping supplies. Be sure to personalize the front with an appliquéd name or label it with the intended contents.

PROJECT
Zippered Shaving Kit with Plastic Lining

MATERIALS:

½ yard beige corduroy
½ yard fleece
½ yard lightweight white plastic lining
¾ yard ½"-wide flat middy braid
½ yard 1"-wide blue grosgrain ribbon
One 11" blue zipper

DIRECTIONS:

Cutting. Cut the following pieces from the corduroy, fleece, and the plastic lining: two 5 " × 5 " end pieces and one 12 " × 16 " bag body. Cut two 3 " × 6 " end handles from the corduroy, placing the 6 " dimension lengthwise on the ribs of the corduroy.

Bag Body. Layer the fleece between the corduroy and the plastic so the right sides are out. Baste all raw edges together, using a ¼ " seam allowance.

Handles. With right sides together, fold each handle piece in half lengthwise, matching the 6 " edges. Stitch and trim the seam allowances to ¼ ". Turn the handles right side out and press them flat so that the seam is at one side edge. Baste the handles to the center of the end pieces, matching the raw edges and allowing the excess handle length to form an arc. The handle is placed so that the corduroy ribs on the handles run parallel to the corduroy ribs on the end pieces. Make sure the nap on the handles and end pieces is in the same direction.

Zipper. Overcast the 12 " edges of the bag body. Position the middy braid on the bag body along both 12 " edges. The edge of the middy braid is ½ " in from the overcast edge. Edgestitch in place.

Stitch the zipper to the bag, lapping the zipper tape ¼ " over the 12 " edge. Repeat for the other side of the zipper.

Position the grosgrain ribbon over the zipper tape and middy braid. The middy braid should extend ¼ " beyond the grosgrain ribbon. Edgestitch the ribbon in place. Repeat on the other edge of the zipper.

Finishing. Attach the ends to the bag body following the directions given under the Duffle Bags in Chapter 3. The shaving kit has square corners on the end pieces instead of rounded corners. To accommodate the change, clip the bag body at the corners so the fabric will pivot at the corner. The end pieces should be attached so that the handles are horizontal.

▶ HINT. Use this convenient bag to hold all the items that fill up the glove compartment of the car. It's ideal for road maps, extra tape cassettes, flashlights. It fits perfectly, tucked under the front seat out of the way.

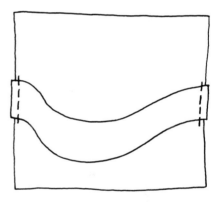

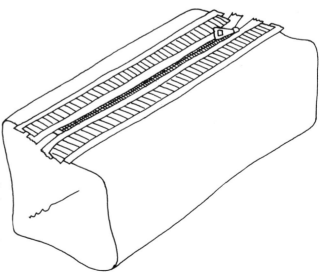

Eyeglass Cases to Make with Cutout Initials

MATERIALS:

⅛ yard gray or tan imitation suede for the outside
⅛ yard burgundy or red imitation suede for the inside
1 ″ Gothic letter stencils
White glue
Thread to match both colors of suede

DIRECTIONS:

Cutting. From both colors of suede, cut one 4″ × 14½″ rectangle. Cut one 3″ × 6″ binding piece from the outside color suede.

Initial. The letter is cut out of the outside color so the inside color is revealed through the opening. Make marks on each side edge of the rectangle 7½″ from one 4″ end. Draw a chalk line across the rectangle, connecting the 2 marks. This is the bottom fold line. The shorter side is the front side.

On the front side, position the initial 1″ up from the bottom fold line and 1″ in from the right side edge. Refer to the instructions for drawing and transferring letters in Chapter 1. Remove the stencil bridges from the letter. Use a tiny, sharp pair of embroidery scissors to cut the letter out along the outline.

Assembly. The upper right corner of the front is rounded. Draw this curve on the outside color rectangles. Working flat, position a small saucer so the curved edges meet the 2 adjacent straight edges of the upper right corner. Draw around the saucer and cut on the line.

Apply a small amount of glue around the letter on the *wrong* side of the outside color. Place the wrong side of the inside and outside colors together, matching raw edges. Press the area around the letter together. Carefully remove any excess glue and allow to dry thoroughly.

Trim the upper right corner of the inside color to match the outside curve. Baste all outer raw edges together ⅛″ from the edge. Match the right side of one edge of the front binding to the wrong side of the curved corner. Ease the binding around the curve. Baste them together and then machine-stitch, using a ¼″ seam allowance.

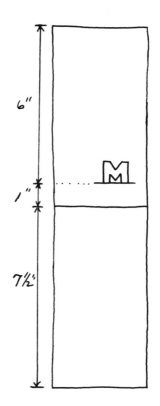

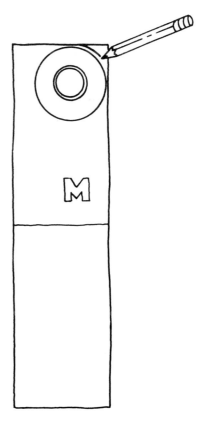

Wrap the binding to the front side, easing it around the curve. Baste and topstitch it in place so a ½″ binding is formed. Trim any excess binding off even with the side edges of the case.

For the pinked version, use pinking shears to pink the binding ⅛″ away from the stitching. For the fringed version, cut the binding off evenly ¾″ from the stitching. Make cuts in the ¾″ edge up to the stitching, at ⅛″ intervals. Be careful not to snip the stitching.

With the right sides out, fold the case in half along the chalk line. Match the side raw edges and baste them together, using a ⅛″ seam allowance.

With matching thread, topstitch the upper straight edge and corners of the case ¼″ from the raw edge. Stop stitching at both sides of the bound front edge. Secure the thread ends neatly. Trim the suede evenly to ⅛″ outside the stitching. Topstitch and trim the side edges in the other color through all thicknesses in the same manner. Reinforce the upper edges of the front at the binding edge.

▶ **Hint.** This case is the perfect size for organizing small objects. Make it as a pencil, checkbook, or calculator case for your favorite executive to tuck into his briefcase.

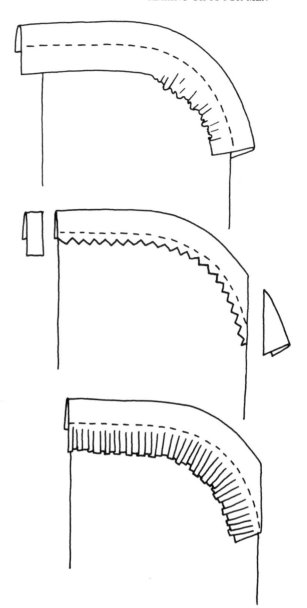

Office Organizer to Tape and Staple with Grasspaper

MATERIALS:

1 yard 18"-wide grasspaper or textured wallpaper
5 yards 1"-wide brown cloth tape
1 yard 18"-wide brown adhesive paper
Standard-size stapler and staples
Three 1½"-wide D-rings in brass finish

DIRECTIONS:

Cutting. Cut the pieces for the organizer from *both* the grasspaper and the adhesive paper. Cut the grasspaper so that the textured strands run horizontally on the cut pieces.

One 18"W × 15"H base piece
One 18"W × 9"H large pocket
One 18"W × 4½"H small pocket
Three 1¼"W × 4"H hanging loops

Backing. Each piece of grasspaper is backed with adhesive paper to make the organizer more durable. Follow the manufacturer's instructions to remove the backing and apply the pieces of adhesive paper to the wrong side of each corresponding grasspaper piece. Trim the edges of the adhesive paper so they are even with the edges of the grasspaper.

Pockets. The top edge of each pocket is finished with cloth tape. Pull about 20" of tape from the roll. Center the tape along the top edge of the small pocket so that half the width of the tape (about ½") is placed on the grasspaper. Press the tape to the grasspaper. Turn the pocket over and fold the tape in half onto the adhesive paper. Press it in place. If the tape does not stick to the grasspaper well, apply a fine stream of white glue between the grasspaper and the tape and press in place. Allow to dry thoroughly. Repeat this on the top edge of the large pocket.

Position the small pocket on top of the large pocket, matching the bottom and side raw edges. The grasspaper sides face up. Use paper clips to hold the raw edges together. The small pocket is divided into 3 compartments. Working from the side edge, insert the 2 pockets into the stapler

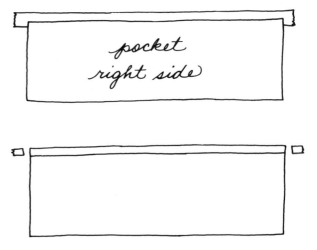

at the taped top of the small pocket. Push the pockets into the stapler as far as possible (about 4½"). Position the stapler over the tape and staple through all thicknesses. Move the stapler down slightly and staple again directly next to the first staple. Repeat this until the row of staples reaches the bottom edge. Repeat this on the opposite side of the small pocket.

The row of staples is covered by a piece of brown tape. Cut a 4½" length of tape that is squared off evenly at both ends. Center it vertically over one row of staples. Press it in place or glue if necessary. Repeat this on the other row of staples.

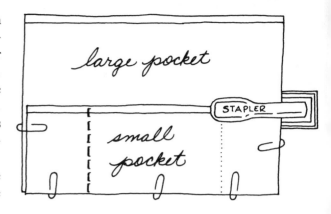

Assembly. The combined pockets are placed on top of the base piece so that the side and bottom edges all match. All grasspaper sides face up. Secure the pockets to the base piece with staples along the side and bottom edges. Place the staples so they are ¼" in from and parallel to the cut edges. Space them next to each other as you did for the small pocket dividers.

Finish the top and bottom edges of the organizer with tape as you did on the pockets. Finish the side edges last, trimming the tape off neatly at the corners. The tape will cover the staples.

Apply tape to each side of the hanging loops in the same manner. Fold each loop in half through a D-ring. Match the cut edges of the grasspaper and staple them together. The 3 loops are positioned along the top edge of the organizer so that the cut edges are on the back side and the loops extend 1" above the top of the organizer. Make sure all the loops are even. Working from the front, staple them exactly at the inside edge of the tape so that the staples are barely noticeable. Place 2 staples through each loop.

Position the organizer upon the wall as desired. Mark the placement for 3 tacks or hooks on the wall. Install the tacks and hang the organizer from the D-rings.

► **HINT.** When new wallpaper is installed use the leftovers to make an organizer that will blend in perfectly to the surroundings. This design is also great for organizing mail at the front door. Make one up in clear plastic as a message center to organize memos in the kitchen.

Sources

My debt of gratitude would not be complete without mentioning the suppliers and manufacturers who have generously contributed materials for this book. Below is a list of sources that I suggest for their consistently fine-quality products. All of the materials used in *Making Gifts for Men* are from these companies.

Sewing threads, embroidery floss, and knitting yarns:
  Coats and Clark's Sales Corporation
  72 Cummings Point Road
  Stamford, Connecticut 06902

Bias tape and trimmings:
  Wrights' Home Sewing Company
  West Warren, Massachusetts 01092

Imitation suede:
  Skinner Fabrics—Ultrasuede®
  Springs Retail & Specialty Fabrics
    Division
  1430 Broadway
  New York, New York 10018

Broadcloth, wools, and duck fabrics:
  Springs Retail & Specialty Fabrics
    Division
  1430 Broadway
  New York, New York 10018

Ribbons:
  C. M. Offray and Son, Inc.
  261 Madison Avenue
  New York, New York 10016

Interfacings:
  Pellon Corporation
  119 West 40th Street
  New York, New York 10018

Batting, fleece, and stuffing:
  Fairfield Processing Corporation
  88 Rose Hill Avenue P.O. Drawer 1157
  Danbury, Connecticut 06810

Fabric fuser:
  Stacy Fabrics Corporation
  38 Passaic Street
  Wood-Ridge, New Jersey 07075

Dyes:
  CPC North America
  RIT Consumer Service Laboratory
  1437 West Morris Street
  Indianapolis, Indiana 46206

Sewing machines:
  Bernina
  Swiss-Bernina, Inc.
  534 West Chestnut
  Hinsdale, Illinois 60521

Printed fabrics:
  Concord Fabrics, Inc.
  1411 Broadway
  New York, New York 10018

Hardware and findings:
  Tandy Leather Company
  P.O. Box 791
  Fort Worth, Texas 76101

Canvas:
  Jensen-Lewis Company, Inc.
  89 Seventh Avenue
  New York, New York 10011

Nylon fabrics:
  Fabri-Quilt
  901 East 14th Avenue P.O. Box
    12479
  North Kansas City, Missouri 64116

Felt:
  Commonwealth Felt Company
  211 Congress Street
  Boston, Massachusetts 02110

LU Felt Patches:
  Lehigh University
  Lehigh Campus
  Bethlehem, Pennsylvania 18018